ZACH NEIL'S

THE NIGHTMARE BEFORE DINNER

RECIPES TO DIE FOR

THE BEETLE HOUSE COOKBOOK

Brimming with creative inspiration, how-to projects, and useful information to enrich your everyday life, Quarto Knows is a favorite destination for those pursuing their interests and passions. Visit our site and dig deeper with our books into your area of interest: Quarto Creates, Quarto Cooks, Quarto Homes, Quarto Lives, Quarto Drives, Quarto Explores, Quarto Gifts, or Quarto Kids.

First published in 2018 by Race Point Publishing, an imprint of The Quarto Group, 142 West 36th Street, 4th Floor, New York, NY 10018, USA

T (212) 779-4972 **F** (212) 779-6058 **www.QuartoKnows.com**

Race Point Publishing titles are also available at discount for retail, wholesale, promotional, and bulk purchase. For details, contact the Special Sales Manager by email at specialsales@quarto.com or by mail at The Quarto Group, Attn: Special Sales Manager, 401 Second Avenue North, Suite 310, Minneapolis, MN 55401, USA.

10 9 8 7 6 5 4 3 2 1

ISBN: 978-1-63106-578-1

Editorial Director: Jeannine Dillon
Managing Editor: Erin Canning
Project Editor: Melanie Madden
Cover Design: Sami Christianson
Interior Design: Melissa Gerber

(Food Photography: Vinnie Finn photography except as noted below)
Food Stylist: Chef Dane Hiett
Beetle House restaurant photos on pages 10, 11, and 154 provided courtesy of Beetle House
Shutterstock images © pages 46, 130, 134, 136, 137, 140, 142, 143, 146, 147, and 153

Printed in China

ZACH NEIL'S

THE NIGHTMARE BEFORE DINNER

RECIPES TO DIE FOR

THE BEETLE HOUSE COOKBOOK

Beetle House
NY. LA

Race Point
PUBLISHING

CONTENTS

Chapter 3: Herbs, Plants & Cauldrons

Chapter 4: Platos de los Muertos

Chapter 5: Tricks & Treats

Chapter 6: Poisons, Potions & Elixirs

Chapter 7: Put the FUN Back in Funeral

Introduction

THIS IS HALLOWEEN

First off, thank you so much for buying this book. No matter who you are or where you are, you have made a difference in my life and made one of my dreams possible. Always believe in yourself and be positive. That is how this book became a reality.

Once upon a time, I was a child from a tiny town, brought up with very humble means. Raised in a religious family that didn't allow the celebration of Halloween, I dreamed of that amazing day when people dress up, express themselves, and, of course, get tricked or treated! To me, the excitement, fright, and fun of Halloween was only a dream, as it was forbidden to me. When I finally reached the age when I could make my own decision about celebrating Halloween, I exposed myself to movies, music, and other art that inspired me, changed my life, and, of course, made me want to open a place where Halloween was celebrated every day. That place now exists, and it's called Beetle House.

As a child, I loved to cook, and my love for food has never waned. During my years as a young musician, I cooked in restaurants to pay the bills when I wasn't on tour. I worked with my closest friends, favorite chefs, and mixologists to craft and create the dishes at my restaurants that not only pay tribute to autumn, my favorite time of year, but also conjure up visions of autumn in the Northeastern United States. The flavors remind me of the change in seasons, good times spent with loved ones, and feasting on stick-to-your-guts, hearty comfort foods. The best part about this odyssey is that I became more interested in plant-based and healthy eating, and was able to craft a vegan alternative for almost every dish on the menu, as well as some perfectly delicious stand-alone vegan dishes. This book is the culmination of my passions.

Enjoy this book, try every recipe, come visit me at one of the Beetle House locations, and most importantly, express yourself every day as if it were Halloween. Be your most authentic self, wear what you want, be who you want—every day is Halloween!

Beetle House Must-Haves

Every chef or good cook knows how important it is to have a well-stocked kitchen! Here are a few essential tools and ingredients for creating your very own dark, evil, and downright frightful food and drink.

TOOLS

Blender or food processor
Baking sheet
Baking pan
Cocktail shaker
Frying pan
Sauté pan
Whisk

INGREDIENTS

Apple cider vinegar
Avocado oil
Bell peppers
Butter
Cayenne pepper
Cheddar cheese
Corn grits
Garlic paste
Garlic powder
Grapeseed/canola oil blend*

Honey
Lemon juice
Olive oil
Rosemary, fresh and dried
Salt and pepper
Smoked paprika
Soy sauce
Sriracha sauce
Worcestershire sauce
Yellow corn

*If you can't find the store-bought version of this oil blend, mix equal parts of grapeseed oil and canola oil to make your own blend.

Veganize It! Wicked Plant-Based Swaps

For most recipes in this book I have included a vegan counterpart, so you can keep it dark and plant-based, too. Believe me: Even if you don't have a Whole Foods, Trader Joe's, or other artisanal grocery on your block, if you have an internet connection, you can veganize anything!

INGREDIENT	VEGAN SUBSTITUTE
Honey	Agave nectar
Sour cream	Tofutti Better Than Sour Cream
Cream cheese	Vegan cream cheese, such as Daiya, Tofutti, or Follow Your Heart
Mayonnaise	Vegan mayo, such as Follow Your Heart Vegenaise
Butter	Vegan butter, such as Earth Balance, or coconut oil
Cheese	Vegan blocks, slices, and shreds, such as Daiya or Follow Your Heart
Worcestershire sauce	Soy or teriyaki sauce
Chicken stock	Vegetable stock
Eggs	Follow Your Heart VeganEgg or mashed banana
Milk	Unsweetened almond or coconut milk
Whipped cream	So Delicious CocoWhip
Ground beef	Tempeh or meatless crumbles
Steak	Portobello or mixed mushrooms

CHAPTER

1

SAUCES & DIPS FOR THE RECENTLY DECEASED

～ Love It Sauce ～

Love It Sauce is a play on a basic Alfredo sauce, and it's very easy to make. Use it for a variety of dishes, including pasta, chicken, beans, and even risotto. I also frankenstein it up to be the main sauce for the Love It Pot Pie (page 78).

DEADLY INGREDIENTS

2 cups (475 ml) heavy whipping cream

1 teaspoon finely chopped fresh
   rosemary

¼ teaspoon crushed garlic
   or garlic paste

1 teaspoon dried parsley

2 cups (200 g) finely grated
   Romano cheese, such as Locatelli

1 tablespoon cream cheese

1 tablespoon butter, softened
   (optional, see Tip)

1 tablespoon all-purpose flour
   (optional, see Tip)

whole milk or cream
   (optional, see Tip)

TO MAKE IT

1. Pour the cream into a medium saucepan. Add the rosemary, garlic, and parsley. Reduce heat, continue to cook for 3 to 5 minutes, whisking constantly. Heat the mixture on medium until it starts to slowly boil.

2. Reduce the heat to low–medium. While whisking constantly, gradually add the Romano cheese. Continue to whisk until the cheese melts and blends into the cream, and the sauce becomes smooth.

3. Add the cream cheese and whisk until blended. If needed, adjust the thickness of sauce (see Tip).

4. Once the sauce has achieved the desired consistency, remove it from the heat. You're done!

TIP If the sauce is too thin, mix together 1 tablespoon softened butter and 1 tablespoon flour to make a roux. Then briskly whisk the roux into the sauce until it thickens. If your sauce is too thick, slowly whisk in a little bit (1 tablespoon at a time) of whole milk or more cream.

Edward Sauce

As the name implies, this sauce is used on our famous Edward Burger Hands (page 62) dish at Beetle House, but this cream-based sriracha sauce is also perfect for dipping French fries and spreading on sandwiches, particularly chicken or burgers. Just like Edward, though, this sauce is too good to last in our world. Make a jar, and Edward Sauce will last for 3 to 4 weeks in the refrigerator.

DEADLY INGREDIENTS

2 cups (460 g) sour cream
2 cups (450 g) mayonnaise
2 tablespoons sugar
½ tablespoon salt
½ tablespoon garlic powder
1 teaspoon smoked paprika
1 teaspoon black pepper
2 tablespoons lime juice
¼ cup (60 ml) sriracha sauce
1 tablespoon chipotle-
  cinnamon spice rub,
  such as Lawry's

TO MAKE IT

1. Place all the ingredients in a bowl and whisk the shit out of them. Your finished sauce should have the consistency of mayonnaise.

GO VEGAN! Use vegan sour cream instead of sour cream, and vegan mayo instead of mayonnaise.

Sweet Lime Cream Sauce

PREP TIME: 10 MINUTES / YIELD: 2½ CUPS (375 G)

This tasty, easy-to-make sauce is great for drizzling on Latin-inspired dishes like chili and tacos. Try it on the Butcher's Stew (page 56) or as a cool contrast to a spicy dish.

DEADLY INGREDIENTS

2 cups (460 g) sour cream
½ cup (120 ml) lime juice
¼ cup (50 g) sugar
½ teaspoon garlic powder
½ teaspoon salt

TO MAKE IT

1. Mix all ingredients in a bowl, whisking briskly until they are fully blended.

2. Store the sauce in a squeeze bottle in the refrigerator.

GO VEGAN! Use vegan sour cream (such as Tofutti) instead of sour cream.

Veruca Sauce

Just like Veruca herself, this sauce has *everything*—a rich, buttery honey taste with a smack of sweet, salt, and garlic all in one! Use it to coat wings, brush over chicken or fish, or douse on anything else you want to give a rich indulgent taste!

DEADLY INGREDIENTS

½ cup (1 stick or 112 g)
  butter, melted

¼ cup (60 ml) chicken stock

1 teaspoon crushed garlic
  or garlic paste

2 teaspoons honey

Salt, to taste

TO MAKE IT

1. Mix all ingredients in a small saucepan. Heat on medium for 5 to 7 minutes, stirring frequently until the butter starts to boil and brown.

2. Remove from the heat and stir.

GO VEGAN! Use vegan butter instead of butter, veggie stock instead of chicken stock, and agave nectar instead of honey.

Hollow Sauce

PREP TIME: 10 MINUTES / YIELD: 1¼ CUPS (300 G)

The Beetle House's Hollow Sauce—also called Gochujang Glaze—is a combination of homemade ketchup and gochujang, which is a Korean fermented chili paste. It's great on chicken, fish, and shellfish, and we use it on our Shrimpy Hollow dish (page 80).

DEADLY INGREDIENTS

¾ cup (180 g) Homemade Ketchup (recipe below)

½ cup (125 g) gochujang

HOMEMADE KETCHUP

Yield: 2 cups

3 cans or jars (6 ounces or 170 g each) organic tomato paste

½ cup (120 ml) apple cider vinegar

1 teaspoon garlic powder

1 tablespoon onion powder

2 tablespoons honey

2 tablespoons molasses

1 teaspoon sea salt

1 teaspoon mustard powder

1 cup (235 ml) water

TO MAKE IT

1. To make the ketchup: Add all of the ingredients to a blender or food processor. Blend on high for 2 to 3 minutes. Place the mixture in an airtight quart jar and refrigerate to let the flavors meld, at least two hours or up to overnight.

2. Whisk the ketchup and gochujang together until smooth.

GO VEGAN! Use agave nectar instead of honey.

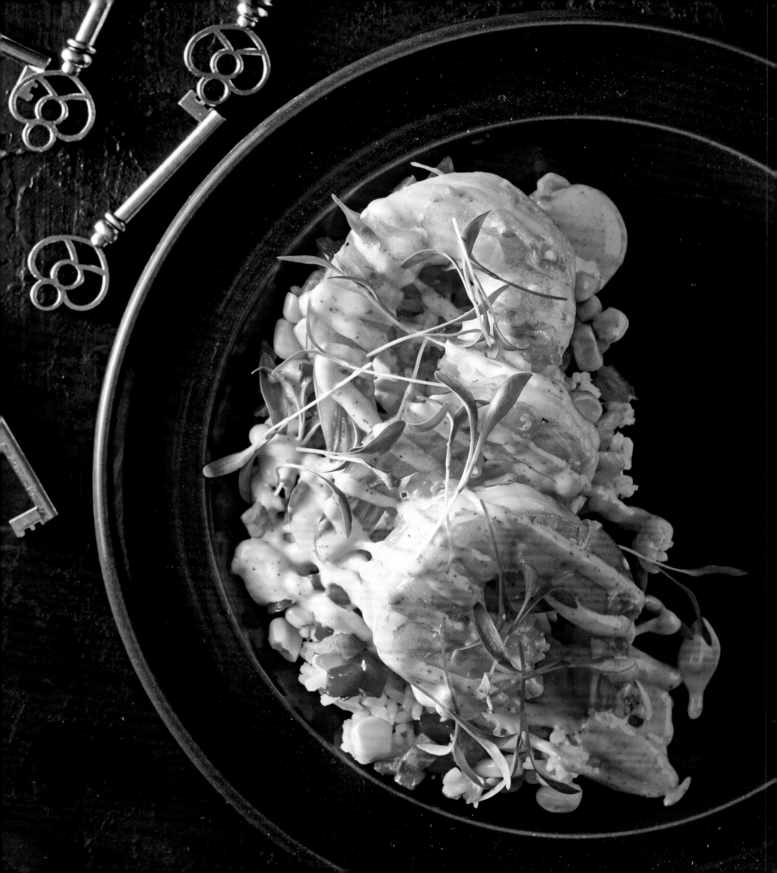

Dead Sauce

PREP TIME: 10 MINUTES | COOK TIME: 5 MINUTES | YIELD: 1¼ CUPS (285 G)

This super-tasty citrus sauce is spicy, sweet, and garlicky. I use it for our Evil Dead Shrimp (page 83), but it also works in a variety of other dishes. Put it in a squeeze bottle and drizzle it over seafood, chicken, or even rice or pasta, and anything else you like.

DEADLY INGREDIENTS

½ cup (1 stick or 112 g) butter, melted

2 tablespoons honey

1 teaspoon crushed garlic or garlic paste

½ teaspoon sea salt

¼ cup (60 ml) lime juice

¼ cup (60 g) sour cream

¼ cup (60 g) mayonnaise

½ teaspoon sriracha sauce

TO MAKE IT

1. Combine the butter, honey, garlic, and salt in a small frying pan. Heat on low until the butter melts and begins to bubble. Allow the garlic to turn golden, but do not overcook. Heat until you get a strong scent of the garlic and butter.

2. Remove the butter mixture from the heat and allow to cool to near room temperature, about 15 minutes.

3. Add the butter mixture and the remaining ingredients to a food processor, and process until smooth and creamy, about 2 minutes.

4. Store the sauce in the refrigerator.

TIP This sauce is best served at room temperature, so remove it from the refrigerator well before your meal.

GO VEGAN! Use vegan butter, vegan sour cream, vegan mayo, and agave nectar.

Cheshire Sauce

PREP TIME: 5 MINUTES | COOK TIME: 20 MINUTES | YIELD: 7 CUPS (1.7 KG)

This famous Beetle House mac and cheese sauce is a favorite, and it also comes in a creamy vegan edition. Serve it over pasta or chicken or use it to make a great queso dip… just add salsa!

DEADLY INGREDIENTS

4 cups (946 ml) heavy whipping cream
1 cup (115 g) shredded white Monterey Jack cheese
1 cup (115 g) shredded cheddar cheese
1 cup (115 g) shredded white American cheese
2 teaspoons yellow or spicy brown mustard
½ teaspoon kosher salt
1½ tablespoons Worcestershire sauce

TO MAKE IT

1. Add the heavy cream to a saucepan and heat on medium until the cream starts to bubble.

2. Slowly add the cheese, 1 cup at a time, whisking constantly so that the cheese melts into the cream.

3. Add the mustard, salt, and Worcestershire sauce. Continue to cook and whisk briskly until the sauce has thickened and the cheese has melted completely, 10 to 12 minutes.

Vegan Cheshire Sauce

PREP TIME: 5 MINUTES | COOK TIME: 20 MINUTES | YIELD: 7 CUPS (1.7 KG)

DEADLY INGREDIENTS

2 cups (475 ml) plain unsweetened almond milk

1/2 cup (120 ml) soy creamer, such as Silk

1 tablespoon nutritional yeast

1 tablespoon vegan sour cream, such as Tofutti

2 tablespoons vegan cream cheese, such as Tofutti

3 slices vegan cheese, such as Chao Creamy Original

2 cups (225 g) shredded vegan cheddar cheese, such as Daiya Cheddar Style Shreds

2 cups (225 g) shredded vegan pepper Jack cheese, such as Daiya Pepperjack Style Shreds

4 slices vegan American cheese, such as Follow Your Heart American Style

1 teaspoon yellow or spicy brown mustard

1/2 teaspoon pink salt

3 teaspoons soy sauce

1 1/2 tablespoons cornstarch

TO MAKE IT

1. Add the almond milk and soy creamer to a saucepan and heat on medium until the mixture starts to bubble.

2. Add the nutritional yeast, sour cream, and cream cheese and whisk. Then slowly add the cheese, a little at a time, whisking constantly to make sure the cheese melts.

3. Add the mustard, salt, and soy sauce. Continue to heat and whisk briskly until the sauce has thickened and all of the cheese has melted, about 5 minutes.

4. Add the cornstarch and continue whisking briskly until blended and the sauce is thick and creamy, at least 3 to 5 minutes.

5. Remove from the heat. Serve and enjoy!

Sweeney Sauce

This delectable wine and mushroom cream sauce
is served on our infamous Sweeney Beef (page 66).

DEADLY INGREDIENTS

¼ cup (½ stick or 55 g) butter, salted

¼ cup (60 ml) olive oil (or your favorite
cooking oil)

½ cup (80 g) diced red onion

1 cup (70 g) sliced cremini mushrooms

¼ cup (45 g) roasted red peppers, chopped

1 teaspoon crushed garlic or garlic paste

½ teaspoon salt

½ teaspoon black pepper

2 tablespoons Worcestershire sauce,
such as Lea & Perrins

1 large sprig fresh rosemary

½ cup (120 ml) Cabernet Sauvignon wine

2 tablespoons balsamic vinegar

1 tablespoon honey

TO MAKE IT

1. In a medium frying pan, add the butter, oil, onions,
mushrooms, roasted red peppers, garlic, salt,
pepper, Worcestershire sauce, and rosemary. Cook
over medium heat for about 5 to 7 minutes until
the vegetables are tender.

2. Add the wine, balsamic vinegar, and honey to the
pan. Continue to cook on medium until the sauce
reduces to a syrupy consistency, 5 to 7 minutes,
stirring occasionally to make sure it doesn't burn.

GO VEGAN! Substitute vegan butter, vegan
Worcestershire sauce or teriyaki sauce, and dark
agave nectar.

Beetle Jam

PREP TIME: 10 MINUTES | COOK TIME: 20 MINUTES | YIELD: 1 CUP (320 G)

This sweet and spicy jelly recipe comes from my mom, who is one of the best cooks in the world. It's a jalepeño pepper jelly, and it's great on simple snacks like crackers with cream cheese or slathered on cornbread. We use it on meats like our Victor Van Pork (page 85), but you can even spread this shit onto a tuna sandwich. This stuff is food gold! Please note that you need a boiling-water canner to make this jam, but trust me, it's worth it.

DEADLY INGREDIENTS

2 green bell peppers, minced

1 red bell pepper, minced

8 ounces (227 g) canned diced jalapeño peppers, drained

1½ cups distilled white vinegar

6½ cups (1.3 kg) white sugar

½ teaspoon cayenne pepper

1 container (6 ounces, or 175 ml) liquid pectin

TO MAKE IT

1. In a large stainless-steel saucepan, combine the bell peppers, jalapeños, vinegar, sugar, and cayenne pepper. Cook over medium-high heat, stirring frequently until the mixture begins to boil.

2. Stir in the pectin and boil 5 more minutes, stirring constantly. Skim off any foam, then remove from the heat.

3. Ladle into sterilized mason jars. Seal and process in a boiling-water canner for 5 minutes.

TIP Not sure how to can? Please follow the instructions on your boiling-water canner for use.

Soul Sauce

This is my Southern BBQ-ish sauce, ready to haunt your dreams and steal the soul from your taste buds! Somewhere between a BBQ and basting sauce, it reminds me of some great soul food sauces from my Southern roots. I use it in the Willy Burger (page 65) and Victor Van Pork (page 85) recipes, but it adds a great BBQ flavor to anything. And it's naturally vegan!

DEADLY INGREDIENTS

¼ cup (60 ml) avocado oil

1 sprig fresh rosemary

1 sprig fresh sage

½ teaspoon garlic powder

⅛ teaspoon cayenne pepper

½ teaspoon smoked paprika

½ teaspoon sea salt

¼ cup (60 ml) apple cider vinegar, such as Bragg

1 can (6 ounces, or 170 g) tomato paste

2¼ cups (530 ml) water

½ cup (120 ml) bourbon, preferably Bulleit

½ tangerine, unpeeled

2 tablespoons blackstrap molasses

½ cup (120 ml) pure maple syrup

TO MAKE IT

1. Mix the oil, rosemary, sage, garlic powder, cayenne, paprika, salt, vinegar, tomato paste, and water in a small saucepan.

2. Slowly bring the mixture to a boil over low heat. Then add the bourbon, tangerine, molasses, and maple syrup. Continue to simmer on low for 40 minutes, stirring occasionally.

3. Remove from heat and allow to cool before serving. Refrigerate in an airtight container.

TIP You can refrigerate this sauce in an airtight container for up to 2 weeks.

CHAPTER

2

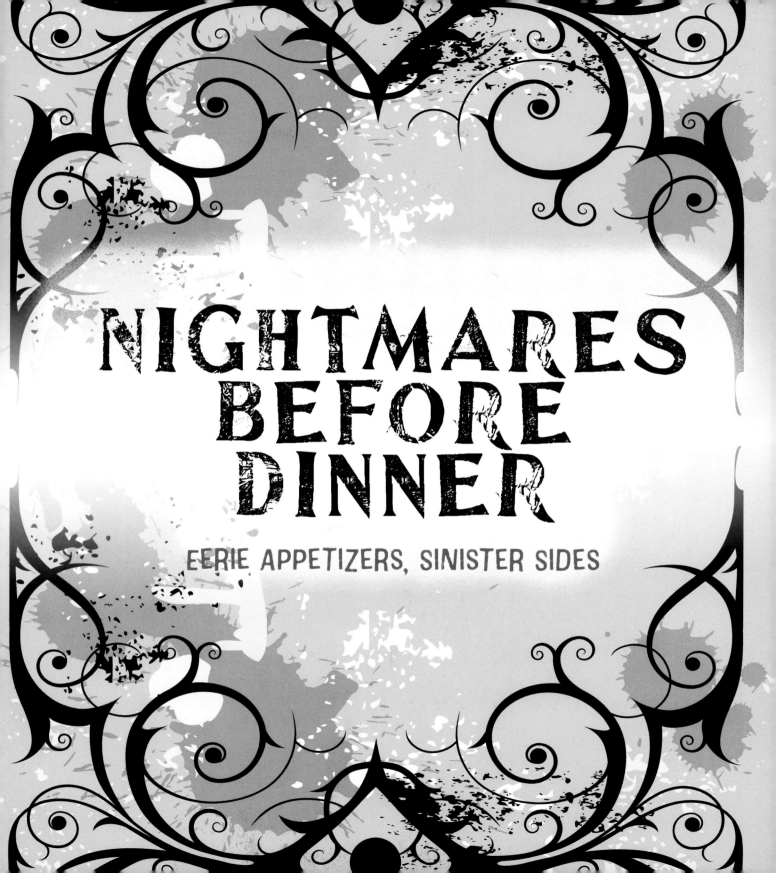

NIGHTMARES BEFORE DINNER

EERIE APPETIZERS, SINISTER SIDES

Brains & Chips

PREP TIME: 15 MINUTES | YIELD: 6 SERVINGS

Cilantro is disgusting! (Okay, if you don't agree with me, that's all right. However, you won't find it in any recipe I create, because I hate it.) So, for this guacamole, you may add it, but I would prefer you didn't. Created for Beetle House NYC, Brains & Chips has been one of our top sellers for the past two years. Serve it in a small bowl or mug. Stick the chips around the edges of the bowl, leaving the center open to garnish with a dash of paprika . . . or some fresh cilantro (if you want to ruin everyone's day).

DEADLY INGREDIENTS

CHIPS

4 moderately ripe plantains
 (firm, not mushy)
¼ cup (75 g) sea salt, for soaking,
 plus more to taste
Coconut oil, for frying
Olive oil, for frying

GUACAMOLE

3 ripe avocados, peeled and pitted
¼ cup (60 ml) lime juice
¼ cup (60 ml) pineapple juice
1 tablespoon honey
½ cup (80 g) chopped red onion
¼ teaspoon chili powder
1 teaspoon sea salt

TIP If the mixture isn't thick enough, add another avocado.

TO MAKE IT

1. **To make the chips:** Peel the plantains and slice them thinly. Place the slices in a bowl of room-temperature water with the salt. Soak the plantain slices for at least 3 hours and up to 24 hours, either at room temperature or in the fridge.

2. After soaking, drain the plantain slices using a paper towel or cloth napkin, making sure they are as dry as possible. In a medium pot, heat a 50–50 blend of coconut and olive oil (or your favorite cooking oil) over medium-high until it reaches an average temperature of 325°F (170°C), 5 to 7 minutes. Using long tongs or a slotted spoon, carefully place the sliced plantains into the oil. Fry the sliced plantains for 5 to 7 minutes until they are golden to medium brown.

3. Remove the plantain chips from the oil and place them into a basket lined with a paper towel to absorb the excess grease. Allow them to cool completely and salt to taste.

4. **To make the guacamole:** Combine all the guacamole ingredients in a food processor and process until smooth and creamy, 2 to 3 minutes.

GO VEGAN! Use agave nectar instead of honey.

The Deetz Shrimp Cocktail

PREP TIME: 10 MINUTES | COOK TIME: 10 MINUTES | YIELD: 4 SERVINGS

This recipe is a flavorful and fun play on the iconic "Deetz" shrimp cocktail served up by Delia Deetz in *Beetlejuice*. Disclaimer: this dish has enough kick to cause a completely unrehearsed but perfectly choreographed dance to the Banana Boat Song. *Day-O!*

DEADLY INGREDIENTS

SHRIMP

4 cups (950 ml) water

½ cup (120 ml) sweetened coconut cream

1 teaspoon salt

¼ cup (60 ml) lime juice

12 jumbo gulf shrimp or prawns, peeled and deveined

Shredded lettuce for garnish

RASPBERRY COCKTAIL SAUCE

½ cup (160 g) seedless raspberry preserve

2 tablespoons sugar

3 tablespoons tomato paste

2 tablespoons Worcestershire sauce

¼ teaspoon garlic powder

½ teaspoon salt

2 tablespoons apple cider vinegar

1 tablespoon horseradish

TO MAKE IT

1. **To make the shrimp:** Combine the water, coconut cream, salt, and lime juice in a pot and bring the mixture to a boil. Add the shrimp and boil until cooked, 5 to 7 minutes. Remove the shrimp with tongs and immediately store in a container in the refrigerator or freezer until cooled.

2. **To make the raspberry cocktail sauce:** Blend all the sauce ingredients in a food processor until very smooth, 2 to 3 minutes. Refrigerate the sauce until cold.

3. Keep the raspberry sauce on the side or pour it directly into your serving dish. Hang the shrimp around the rim of your serving dish in a coupe or cocktail glass if serving individually or all together in a larger serving dish. Garnish with shredded lettuce if desired.

Graveyard Noodles

PREP TIME: 8 MINUTES | COOK TIME: 15 MINUTES | YIELD: 6–8 SERVINGS

This tasty veggie noodle dish will leave you—and even the most discerning meat eaters in your life—happily haunted! Serve it as a sloppy and creepy appetizer or as a "wormy" side to any haunted dish in this book. Garnish with tombstone props, if you like.

DEADLY INGREDIENTS

¼ cup (60 ml) olive oil

1 teaspoon crushed garlic or garlic paste

1 teaspoon fresh chopped rosemary or dried rosemary

½ teaspoon sea salt

⅛ teaspoon cayenne pepper

10 ounces (280 g) fresh-cut zucchini "zoodles" and summer squash "noodles" (see Tip)

1 teaspoon agave nectar

2 tablespoons lime juice

TO MAKE IT

1. Heat the oil in a medium frying pan with the garlic, rosemary, salt, and cayenne until the garlic starts to sizzle.

2. Add the noodles and sauté for 3 to 5 minutes, stirring often.

3. Add the agave and continue to sauté. Add the lime juice and sauté for another 3 minutes, until the noodles start to get tender and the edges become golden.

TIP You can use a spiralizer tool to make squash and zucchini noodles at home, but fresh vegetable noodles are also available in the refrigerated section of most grocery stores.

Diablo's Arenas Crostini (aka Devil's Grits Crostini)

PREP TIME: 5 MINUTES | COOK TIME: 15 MINUTES | YIELD: 6–8 SERVINGS

Cheesy, creamy, rich, spicy, stick-to-your-ribs grits on buttery garlic crostini! A proper temptation for a cold fall or winter night, this dish is a perfect starter or side dish with plenty of Southern flair and just enough spice.

DEADLY INGREDIENTS

GRITS

4 cups (946 ml) milk

½ teaspoon salt

2 teaspoons sriracha sauce

¼ teaspoon garlic powder

¼ teaspoon cayenne pepper

½ cup (25 g) chopped scallions

1 cup (140 g) corn grits

½ cup (50g) grated Parmesan cheese

¾ cup (85 g) shredded cheddar cheese

¾ cup (85 g) shredded American cheese

¼ cup (½ stick or 55 g) butter

CROSTINI

¼ cup (60 ml) olive oil

1 tablespoon chopped garlic or garlic paste

1 large baguette, thinly sliced

TO MAKE IT

1. **To make the grits:** Mix the milk, salt, sriracha, garlic powder, cayenne pepper, scallions, and grits in a medium saucepan. Cook on medium-low heat until creamy and smooth, 12 to 15 minutes. Remove from the heat.

2. Add the cheeses and butter, stir well, and return to medium-low heat for an additional 3 to 5 minutes. Whisk frequently until fully blended.

3. **To make the crostini:** Preheat the oven to 350°F (180°C).

4. Mix the olive oil and garlic paste in a small bowl and brush it all over each slice of bread. Place the bread on a baking sheet and cook for 15 to 20 minutes until crispy and golden brown.

5. Serve the grits in bowls with 2 to 3 crostini around the edges and a single red cocktail fork sticking up out of the center.

Hallowpeño Honey Cheddar Cornbread

PREP TIME: 10 MINUTES | COOK TIME: 30 MINUTES | YIELD: 10 SERVINGS

This cheesy, spicy, and sweet bread started as a complement to my Butcher's Stew (page 56), but it is fantastic as an appetizer or side to any dish. Serve this cornbread as the base for Love It Pot Pie (page 78), as a dipper for soups and stews, or just spread some butter on it and serve.

DEADLY INGREDIENTS

1 box (8.5 ounces, or 240 g) Jiffy Vegetarian Corn Muffin Mix

½ cup (145 g) finely chopped jalapeño peppers (seeds removed)

2 cups (225 g) shredded sharp white cheddar cheese

3 tablespoons honey

1 egg

⅓ cup (80 ml) milk

¼ cup (58 g) sour cream

1½ tablespoons dried rosemary

1 teaspoon smoked paprika

1 can (15.25 ounces, or 432 g) whole-kernel corn, drained

1 tablespoon soy sauce

TO MAKE IT

1. Preheat the oven to 400°F (200°C). Grease an 8-inch (20 cm) square baking pan.

2. Place all of the ingredients in a large mixing bowl and use a whisk or electric mixer to blend them all together until the batter has a grainy texture.

3. Pour the batter into the prepared pan, transfer it to the oven, and bake until golden brown, 20 to 30 minutes.

4. Allow the cornbread to cool for 20 minutes. Then cut it into squares and serve warm with butter or a butter alternative.

GO VEGAN! Substitute your favorite vegan cheddar-style shredded cheese, 1 tablespoon dark agave nectar, vegan egg substitute, unsweetened almond or coconut milk, and vegan sour cream (such as Tofutti).

Charlie Corn Bucket

PREP TIME: 10 MINUTES | COOK TIME: 30 MINUTES | YIELD: 8–10 SERVINGS

With only a 10-minute prep time, this creamy, cheesy casserole dish works
great as an appetizer or side, and the breadcrumbs add some delicious texture.
The vegan version is tasty, too!

DEADLY INGREDIENTS

BREAD CRUMB TOPPING

1/3 cup (60 g) plain bread crumbs

1/4 teaspoon salt

1 teaspoon honey

1/8 teaspoon garlic powder

2 tablespoons melted butter

CHEESE CASSEROLE

1/2 cup (120 ml) half-and-half

1/2 cup (58 g) shredded American cheese

2 heaping tablespoons cream cheese

2 teaspoons soy sauce

1 can (15.25 ounces, or 432 g)
    whole-kernel corn, drained

1 tablespoon cornstarch

1/2 cup (58 g) shredded cheddar cheese

TO MAKE IT

1. **To make the bread crumb topping:** In a small bowl, mix the bread crumbs with the salt, honey, garlic powder, and melted butter until thoroughly mixed and the bread crumbs are moistened.

2. **To make the cheese casserole:** Preheat the oven to 350°F (180°C).

3. Combine the half-and-half, American cheese, and cream cheese in a saucepan and bring the mixture to a boil, whisking constantly until the cheese and cream cheese have melted to form a thicker cheese sauce. Whisk in the soy sauce.

4. Add the corn to the cheese sauce, followed by the cornstarch. Whisk continuously on medium until the mixture is very thick, 3 to 5 minutes. Then remove the mixture from the heat and pour into a small casserole pan.

5. Sprinkle with the shredded cheddar cheese. Then sprinkle the bread crumb mixture over the cheese.

6. Transfer the casserole to the oven and bake until the cheese is fully melted and the bread crumbs are golden brown, about 30 minutes. Remove from the oven and let cool.

GO VEGAN! Substitute agave nectar, vegan butter, dairy-free creamer (such as Silk), 2 slices of American-style vegan cheese (such as Follow Your Heart), vegan cream cheese (such as Tofutti), and vegan cheddar (such as Daiya).

Beetle Bacon Bread

PREP TIME: 30 MINUTES | **COOK TIME:** 12 MINUTES | **YIELD:** 10–15 SERVINGS

This Beetle House NYC original is one of my favorite bread dishes of all time. It's a hearty sundried tomato and bacon "pizza" with a sweet balsamic reduction, soft mozzarella cheese, and crisp scallions. It is to die for, and if you eat too much of it, you just might!

DEADLY INGREDIENTS

BREAD

1 large loaf Italian bread or peasant-style bread, sliced 1 ½ inches (4 cm) thick

BREAD COATING

½ cup (1 stick or 112 g) butter, melted

1 teaspoon chopped garlic or garlic paste

½ teaspoon honey

SPREAD

1 package (13 ounces, or 368 g) sun-dried tomatoes, dry packed

6 strips hickory smoked bacon, cooked (soft, not crispy)

½ cup (120 ml) heavy whipping cream

½ cup (115 g) mayonnaise

1 cup (100 g) finely grated Parmesan cheese

½ teaspoon garlic powder

1 teaspoon dried rosemary

¼ cup (40 g) diced red onion

GLAZE

1 cup (235 ml) balsamic vinegar

¼ cup (50 g) sugar

Pinch sea salt

TOPPINGS

1 to 2 large mozzarella balls or loaves, sliced ½ inch (13 mm) thick

¼ to ½ cup (25 to 50 g) chopped scallions

½ cup (90 g) chopped roasted red peppers

Curly kale for garnish

Parsley for garnish

TO MAKE IT

1. To make the bread coating: Stir the butter, garlic, and honey until combined and set aside.

2. To make the spread: Combine the sun-dried tomatoes, cooked bacon, cream, mayonnaise, Parmesan, garlic powder, rosemary, and onion in a food processor. Process until smooth and creamy. Using a spatula, scrape the spread into a bowl and transfer it to the refrigerator.

3. To make the glaze: Pour the balsamic vinegar, sugar, and salt into a small saucepan. Heat the mixture on medium, stirring occasionally, until the glaze reduces by half and becomes syrupy but not too thick. Remove from heat and allow to cool.

4. Preheat the oven to 350°F (180°C).

5. Meanwhile, brush the bread coating mixture evenly over each slice of bread, making sure to cover it entirely. Place the coated bread slices on a baking sheet and bake them until they start to turn slightly brown, 5 to 7 minutes.

6. Take your spread out of the refrigerator and heat it on the stove for 3 to 5 minutes so it's a little warmer than room temperature. Using a spoon, cover each slice of bread with a generous amount of the spread, so that the coating is ¾ to 1 inch (20 to 25 mm) thick.

7. On top of the spread, place one slice of mozzarella, leaving the edges uncovered and making sure that the cheese covers at least two-thirds of the bread. Place the bread back in the oven and bake until the cheese is melted, 7 to 10 minutes.

8. Drizzle about ½ teaspoon of balsamic glaze over the top of each piece of bread. Then place about a teaspoon of the chopped scallions and roasted red peppers on each piece.

9. Serve the bread on a dark-colored plate. Drizzle additional glaze on the plate and around the bread. Garnish with something green like curly kale or parsley. . . and don't forget the plastic beetles!

TIP Don't allow your cheese to get brown, runny, or crispy. When it is ready, it should be tender and stretchy.

CHAPTER

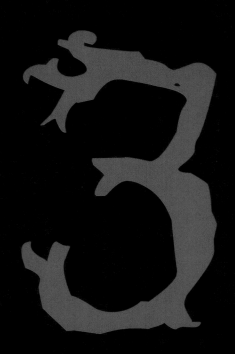

HERBS, PLANTS & CAULDRONS

SOUPS AND SALADS FOR THE LIVING

Sriracha-Roasted Butternut Squash Death Soup

PREP TIME: 10 MINUTES | COOK TIME: 1 HOUR | YIELD: 8–10 SERVINGS

This sweet, hearty, stick-to-your-ribs soup is perfect for a chilly autumn night—it's a warm-you-up, haunt-your-taste buds-and-sing-to-your-soul kind of meal. And the best part is that it's naturally vegan!

DEADLY INGREDIENTS

3 cups (390 g) diced butternut squash

1 cup (160 g) diced red onion

1/3 cup (80 ml) olive oil

1/4 teaspoon ground coriander

1/2 teaspoon ground cinnamon

1/2 teaspoon garlic powder

1/2 teaspoon smoked paprika

1/4 teaspoon ground nutmeg

1/2 teaspoon sea salt

1 cup (235 ml) plain almond milk

1/2 cup (120 ml) vanilla soy milk

1/2 teaspoon sriracha sauce, plus more for serving

1/4 cup (31 g) chopped nuts (any type)

TO MAKE IT

1. Preheat the oven to 400°F (200°C). Place the squash and onion in a roasting pan. Add the olive oil and stir to coat the vegetables, then sprinkle the coriander, cinnamon, garlic powder, smoked paprika, nutmeg, and salt over the top. Cover and roast for 45 minutes.

2. Transfer the roasted squash mixture to the food processor, making sure to get all the drippings, oil, and burnt ends from the pan. Add the almond milk, soy milk, and sriracha and process until smooth and creamy, about 3 minutes.

3. Transfer the mixture to a saucepan and heat on medium until it reaches a slow, rolling boil. Lower the heat for 3 to 5 minutes, until it is at your desired temperature.

4. Divide among bowls. Drizzle with a few drops of sriracha (or tabasco), or more to your taste, and garnish with the chopped nuts.

Fall Salad

PREP TIME: 15 MINUTES / YIELD: 4–6 SERVINGS

This crisp salad—one of my favorite healthy dishes—contains all the flavors of autumn. If you have a small- to medium-sized pumpkin handy, hollow it out and serve the salad inside it. Trust me, your guests will love it, but don't blame me if the Headless Horseman comes knocking.

DEADLY INGREDIENTS

SALAD

1 cup (200 g) chopped butternut squash

2 tablespoons olive oil

1 teaspoon sea salt

½ teaspoon garlic powder

8 cups (160 g) chopped romaine lettuce

¾ cup (112 g) whole-kernel corn

½ cup (90 g) chopped roasted red peppers

½ cup (75 g) dried cranberries

½ cup (63 g) chopped candied walnuts (vegan)

¾ cup (135 g) chopped heirloom tomatoes

¼ cup (40 g) chopped red onion

¼ cup (25 g) shaved radish

1 cup (40 g) seasoned croutons (vegan)

DRESSING

1 cup (235 ml) apple cider (or apple juice)

½ cup (120 ml) apple cider vinegar

2 tablespoons honey

¼ cup (60 ml) olive oil or avocado oil

1 teaspoon salt

½ teaspoon pepper

½ teaspoon chopped garlic or garlic paste

1 teaspoon dried rosemary

TO MAKE IT

1. **To make the salad:** Sauté the butternut squash in a pan with the olive oil, sea salt, and garlic powder until slightly tender, 5 to 7 minutes. Remove from the heat and let cool. Mix the remaining salad ingredients, except for the croutons, in a large salad bowl. Add the cooled squash and combine.

2. **To make the dressing:** Add all the dressing ingredients to a food processor. Process for 2 to 3 minutes, and then toss with the salad.

3. Garnish with the croutons.

Giant Peach Salad

PREP TIME: 30 MINUTES | YIELD: 1 SERVING

This spring mix and frisée salad was created by the brilliant Chef Christoffer Binotto and is tossed with a peach vinaigrette and topped with grilled peaches, shaved radish, micro basil, and crispy fried prosciutto. A drizzle of basil oil adds the perfect finish!

DEADLY INGREDIENTS

BASIL OIL

½ cup (20 g) basil

¼ cup (10 g) spinach

2 cups (475 ml) grapeseed/
canola oil blend

SALAD

5 slices of peach

2 tablespoons (30ml)
grapeseed/canola oil blend

Pinch salt, plus more to garnish

¼ cup Prosciutto,
sliced paper-thin

4 ounces (115 g) Spring mix

2 ounces (50 g) Frisée

5 slices of radish,
sliced paper-thin, for garnish

Micro basil for garnish

5 slices of radish, sliced
paper-thin, for garnish

PEACH VINAIGRETTE

5 whole peaches,
pitted and roughly chopped

¼ cup (60 ml) grapeseed/canola
oil blend

Mango vinegar, such as Huilerie
Beaujolaise, to taste

TO MAKE IT

1. **To make the basil oil:** Quickly blanch the basil and spinach in boiling water for 30 seconds. Remove and transfer the greens to a bowl of ice water to stop the cooking. Drain and squeeze as much liquid from the greens as possible. Mix the greens with the oil blend and, ideally, refrigerate overnight.

2. Strain to remove the greens and discard them.

3. **To make the salad:** Preheat a deep fryer to 325°F (170°C). (If you don't have a deep fryer, use a frying pan with ½ inch, or 13 mm, of cooking oil of your choice.) In a separate medium frying pan, lightly toss the peach slices in 2 tablespoons of the oil blend and a pinch of salt. Grill until tender over medium heat, 2 to 4 minutes. Remove peaches from the heat and set aside.

4. When the deep fryer (or your frying pan with ½ inch, or 13 mm, of cooking oil) is ready, slowly lower each prosciutto slice into the oil and cook until crispy, about 90 seconds. Place the finished slices on a paper towel-lined plate. When cool, chop into small pieces.

5. **To make the peach vinaigrette:** Add the peaches and blend all together. Add mango vinegar to taste.

6. Toss the peach vinaigrette with the spring mix and frisée in a large bowl.

7. Place the grilled peach slices on a plate and cover with the lettuce mixture. Garnish with the radish, micro basil, prosciutto, and salt. Finally, drizzle the basil oil around the edges of the plate.

Barbarous BBQ Beef Ramen

PREP TIME: 20 MINUTES | **COOK TIME:** 30 MINUTES | **YIELD:** 8–10 SERVINGS

There is nothing like a hot and hearty noodle soup on a chilly fall or winter day, and this one is certain to warm your bones and fill your belly. Don't eat meat? Try the equally tasty vegan edition!

DEADLY INGREDIENTS

2 tablespoons avocado oil

4 tablespoons olive oil, reserved

1½ cups (240 g) diced red onion

¼ cup (33 g) chopped carrot

¼ cup (25 g) chopped celery

2 teaspoons fresh grated ginger or ginger paste

¼ teaspoon ground cinnamon

⅛ teaspoon cayenne pepper

1 teaspoon sea salt

2 cups (140 g) sliced shitake mushrooms

1 cup (135 g) chopped yellow squash

2 cups (85 g) chopped kale

2 tablespoons lime juice

1 container (32 ounces, or 946 ml) chicken stock

1 tablespoon honey

11 cups (2.6 L) water, divided

12 ounces (355 ml) organic teriyaki sauce

2 tablespoons ketchup

¼ cup (65 g) barbecue sauce

¼ teaspoon sriracha sauce

¼ cup (25 g) chopped scallions

1 pound (454 g) ground beef

1 package (about 1 pound, or 454 g) ramen or udon noodles, cooked according to package instructions

5 soft-boiled eggs, cut in half, to garnish

TO MAKE IT

1. Pour the avocado oil and 2 tablespoons of the olive oil into a large pot. Add the onion, carrot, celery, ginger, cinnamon, cayenne, and sea salt, and sauté over medium heat for 3 minutes.

2. Add the mushrooms, squash, kale, and lime juice. Continue to sauté for another 3 minutes. Add the stock, honey, and 8 cups (1.9 L) of the water. Bring the mixture to a boil over high heat and boil for 10 minutes.

3. Stir in the teriyaki sauce and the remaining 3 cups (700 ml) of water. Continue to boil for 10 more minutes, stirring often.

4. In a frying pan over medium heat, add the remaining 2 tablespoons olive oil, the ketchup, barbecue sauce, sriracha, and scallions. Add the ground beef and sauté until cooked, about 5 to 7 minutes.

5. Put a hearty amount of noodles into each bowl. Ladle broth and veggies over the top, until you have soupy mixture. Divide the meat between the bowls, placing it to the side. Garnish with half a soft-boiled egg on top.

GO VEGAN! Substitute vegetable stock, agave nectar, and meatless crumbles.

✒ The Butcher's Stew ✒

PREP TIME: 25 MINUTES | COOK TIME: 4 HOURS | YIELD: 12-16 SERVINGS

The base of this classic, New York firehouse-style chili recipe was shared with me by a friend who works at New York Ladder. I, of course, doctored it to be a bit darker and more evil! Depending on how meaty you want the chili, you can add more or less ground beef to your version, but make sure you cook it on that low steady temperature for a few hours to let the flavors soak in.

DEADLY INGREDIENTS

2 tablespoons olive oil

1 red bell pepper, diced

1 green bell pepper, diced

2 large red onions, diced

2 to 4 pounds (907 g to 1.8 kg) ground beef (see headnote)

1 teaspoon crushed garlic or garlic paste

3 tablespoons chili powder

1½ tablespoons ground cumin

1 teaspoon ground cinnamon

2 tablespoons sriracha sauce

1 teaspoon salt

1 teaspoon black pepper

1 teaspoon Cajun seasoning

2 tablespoons sugar

2 large cans (23 ounces, or 660 g each) tomato soup

4 cans (14.5 ounces, or 411 g, each) stewed tomatoes

15 ounces (1¾ cups, or 425 g) canned crushed tomatoes

2 cans (15.25 ounces, or 432 g, each) whole-kernel corn, drained

2 cans (15 ounces, or 425 g, each) kidney beans

2 cans (15 ounces, or 425 g, each) black beans, drained

Chopped scallion greens, for serving

Shredded cheddar or vegan cheddar-style cheese, for serving

TO MAKE IT

1. Heat the olive oil in a large saucepan over medium for about 3 minutes. Then add the chopped bell peppers and onions. Sauté for 3 minutes.

2. Add the ground beef, garlic, chili powder, cumin, cinnamon, and sriracha. Continue to cook until the meat is browned, about 5 minutes.

3. Add the salt, pepper, Cajun seasoning, and sugar. Stir to combine thoroughly.

4. After the meat and veggies are cooked, add the tomato soup and stewed tomatoes. (Use a large spoon or potato smasher and try to smash up the stewed tomatoes.) Then add the crushed tomatoes, corn, and beans. Cook on low heat for at least 2 hours (or up to 3 hours for maximum flavor).

5. To serve, divide the stew among bowls. Drizzle with a swirl of Sweet Lime Cream Sauce (page 18), and sprinkle with fresh chopped scallions and a little shredded cheese. Serve with a piece of Hallowpeño Honey Cheddar Cornbread (page 41).

GO VEGAN! Use tempeh or meatless crumbles in lieu of ground beef.

CHAPTER

4

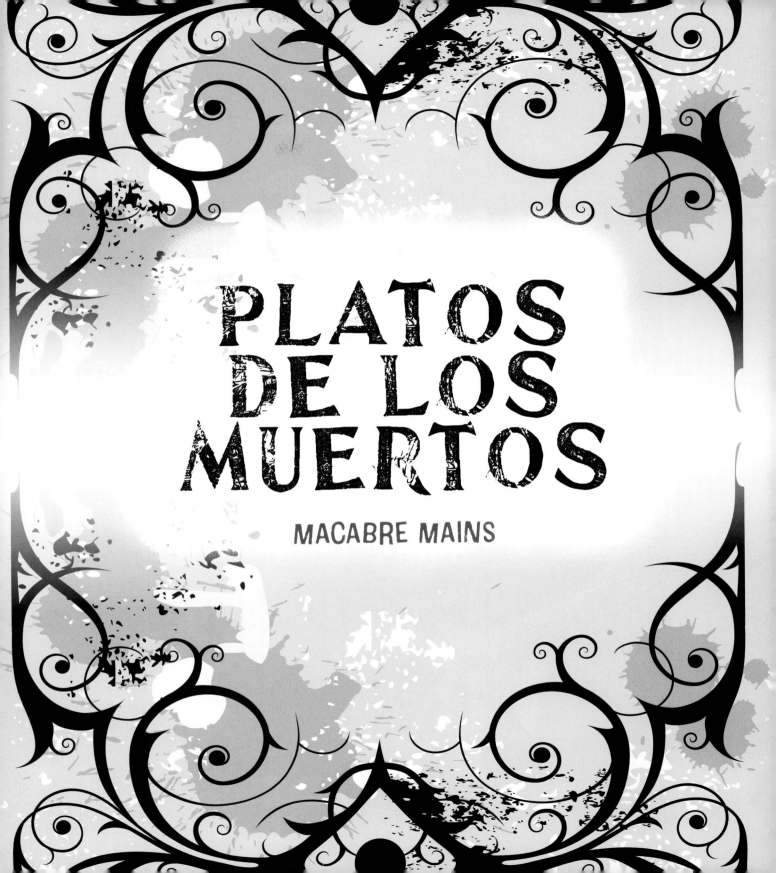

PLATOS DE LOS MUERTOS

MACABRE MAINS

Cheshire Mac and Cheese

PREP TIME: 10 MINUTES | COOK TIME: 12 MINUTES | YIELD: 8–10 SERVINGS

This sweet-and-spicy take on one of America's beloved comfort foods is a Beetle House favorite! In keeping with the "Alice's Tea Party" theme, try serving this creamy dish in large teacups instead of bowls. Or you can just serve it in a skull like we did!

DEADLY INGREDIENTS

CHESHIRE SAUCE

See page 24, to taste

SWEET STEWED TOMATO

1 can (14.5 ounces, or 411 g) organic stewed tomatoes
¼ teaspoon garlic powder
½ teaspoon salt
1 tablespoon honey

BREAD CRUMB TOPPING

2 tablespoons butter, salted
½ cup (60 g) plain bread crumbs
¼ teaspoon salt
¼ teaspoon black pepper
⅛ teaspoon garlic powder

PASTA

1 pound (454 g) medium-shell pasta

TO MAKE IT

1. To make the sweet stewed tomato: In a medium saucepan, combine the stewed tomatoes with the garlic powder, salt, and honey. Bring the mixture to a boil for 3 to 5 minutes on medium heat, crushing the tomatoes as much as you can with a whisk.

2. To make the bread crumb topping: In a small saucepan, melt the butter and then add the bread crumbs, salt, pepper, and garlic powder, mixing until the bread crumbs are moist.

3. Cook the pasta shells in boiling water according to the package instructions. Strain.

4. Preheat the broiler to 500°F (260°C).

5. In a large frying pan, heat the Cheshire Sauce on medium until it has a thin, liquid consistency. Add the pasta and mix until evenly coated. Pour the cheesy pasta into a broiler-safe dish and sprinkle with the Bread Crumb Topping.

6. Broil until the bread crumbs are golden brown, 2 to 4 minutes.

7. To serve, divide the casserole between plates and pour 2 tablespoons of Sweet Stewed Tomato over the top of each dish.

GO VEGAN! Substitute Cheshire Sauce: Vegan Edition (page 24), agave nectar, and vegan butter.

Edward Burger Hands

PREP TIME: 10 MINUTES / COOK TIME: 15 MINUTES / YIELD: 1 SERVING

This is where it all began: Beetle House's very first recipe. I wanted to make a burger with a lot of different parts, just like Edward Scissorhands. After some experimenting, Edward Burger Hands was born. This burger is absolutely overflowing with seven layers, and the only way we could figure out how to keep it closed was to shove a pair of scissors right through it. Edward is always an inspiration!

DEADLY INGREDIENTS

EGG, SUNNY-SIDE UP

½ tablespoon butter
1 egg

BURGER

Pinch of salt and black pepper
Pinch of garlic powder
Pinch of ground cinnamon
1 burger patty (8 ounces, or 227 g)
1 slice Pepper Jack cheese
1 burger bun
2 strips bacon, fried
1 piece romaine lettuce
1 slice tomato
2 slices avocado
2 large pieces roasted red peppers

VERUCA SAUCE

See page 20, to taste

EDWARD SAUCE

See page 17, to taste

TO MAKE IT

1. **To make the egg, sunny-side up:** In a small frying pan, dissolve the butter on medium heat. Then crack open an egg and add it to the pan, cooking until the whites are set and the yolks are cooked to desired doneness, about 4 to 5 minutes.

2. **To make the burger:** In a small bowl, mix together equal parts salt, pepper, garlic powder, and cinnamon. In a large bowl, add the burger patty and the seasoning mixture, pressing the mixture into the patty until it is seasoned. Don't overdo it here, just make sure the patty is coated.

3. For a rare patty, cook in a small frying pan over medium heat for 2½ minutes per side. For a well-done patty, cook for 5 minutes on each side. Then add the cheese and cook until it is melted. Remove from the heat.

4. Brush the inside of both the top and bottom bun with a hearty amount of Veruca Sauce, then toast the bun in the pan or in a toaster oven for about 3 to 5 minutes, or cook until it is golden brown.

5. Spread the Edward Sauce on the inside of the bottom bun, and then place the patty on top. On top of the burger, place the egg, and then the bacon. Using a squirt bottle, decorate the top with Edward Sauce.

6. On the top bun, add the lettuce, tomato, avocado, and roasted red peppers. Serve with sides of your choosing.

The Willy Burger

PREP TIME: 10 MINUTES | COOK TIME: 15 MINUTES | YIELD: 1 SERVING

A sweet and succulent, over-the-top burger, as wild as Wonka himself. This is a great summertime treat, but it can of course be made year-round. Serve it on a white plate drizzled with chocolate syrup, and don't worry if you can't find candied or chocolate-covered bacon; you can sauté the bacon with brown sugar instead to candy it.

DEADLY INGREDIENTS

BURGER

Pinch of salt and black pepper
Pinch of garlic powder
Pinch of ground cinnamon
1 burger patty (8 ounces, or 227 g)
1 burger bun
1 slice of smoked cheddar cheese
Handful French-fried onions,
  store-bought
2 strips chocolate-covered
  or candied bacon
1 ring pineapple
1 piece romaine
1 slice tomato

VERUCA SAUCE

See page 20, to taste

SOUL SAUCE

See page 30, to taste

BEETLE JAM

See page 29, to taste

TO MAKE IT

1. **To make the burger:** In a small bowl, mix together equal parts salt, pepper, garlic powder, and cinnamon. In a large bowl, add the burger patty and the seasoning mixture, pressing the mixture into the patty until it is seasoned.

2. For a rare patty, cook in a small frying pan over medium heat for 2½ minutes per side. For a well-done patty, cook for 5 minutes on each side. Then add the cheese and until it is melted. Remove from the heat.

3. Brush the inside of both the top and bottom bun with a hearty amount of Veruca Sauce. Place the buns, sauce side down, in the pan or toaster oven for about 3 to 5 minutes or until golden brown. Grill the pineapple in a pan until browned around the edges, approximately 2 minutes per side.

4. Spread the Soul Sauce on the bottom bun and place the cooked burger patty on top. Cover with a handful of French-fried onions. Then add the bacon and grilled pineapple.

5. Spread Beetle Jam on the top bun. Then top with lettuce and tomato. Using a squirt bottle, decorate with a liberal amount of Soul Sauce. Serve with a side of your choice.

～ Sweeney Beef ～

PREP TIME: 10 MINUTES | COOK TIME: 15 MINUTES | YIELD: 2 SERVINGS

If the Demon Barber had a favorite steak, this would be it. To up the creepy factor, splatter the sauce to resemble blood and serve the dish with a straight shaving razor, which conveniently doubles as a steak knife.

DEADLY INGREDIENTS

STEAK

1 tablespoon butter, softened

2 filets mignon (8 ounces, or 227 g, each)

Pinch salt and pepper

Pinch garlic powder

Pinch ground cinnamon

GARLIC MASH

4 medium russet potatoes

2 tablespoons salted butter

1 cup (235 ml) half-and-half or heavy cream

1½ teaspoons salt

2 teaspoons crushed garlic or garlic paste

1 teaspoon sugar

SWEENEY SAUCE

See page 27, to taste

TO MAKE IT

1. **To make the steak:** Coat the outside of each filet with the butter. Then sprinkle each side with a mixture of salt, pepper, garlic powder, and cinnamon. Cook the filets on medium heat in a pan or on a grill (it's your choice, but I recommend pan cooking) to your desired taste, 2½ minutes per side for rare and 5 minutes per side for well-done. Then remove from the heat.

2. **To make the garlic mash:** Peel the potatoes and then cut each into 3 or 4 pieces. Boil them until soft, 15 to 20 minutes.

3. Transfer the potato pieces to another pot or just drain them and put them back in the same pot. Add the butter, half-and-half, salt, crushed garlic, and sugar. Smash with a potato smasher, and then whip with an electric mixer until smooth and creamy.

4. Divide the mash between two plates and place the steaks on top. Garnish with the Sweeney Sauce, spooning a generous amount over the steak. Then splatter the sauce around the dish to resemble splattered blood.

Sweeney Mushroom

PREP TIME: 10 MINUTES | **COOK TIME: 15 MINUTES** | **YIELD: 2 SERVINGS**

DEADLY INGREDIENTS

MUSHROOMS

¼ cup (60 ml) olive oil

1 teaspoon crushed garlic
  or garlic paste

¼ cup (60 ml) lemon juice

2 large Portobello mushroom caps

Salt and pepper, to taste

GARLIC MASH

4 medium russet potatoes

2 tablespoons vegan butter

1 cup (235 ml) unsweetened
  almond or soy milk

1½ teaspoons salt

2 teaspoons crushed garlic
  or garlic paste

1 teaspoon sugar

VEGAN SWEENEY SAUCE

See page 27, to taste

GARNISH

1 small red onion, chopped
  and sautéed

1 red bell pepper, chopped
  and sautéed

micro greens

TO MAKE IT

1. **To make the mushrooms:** Mix together the olive oil, garlic, and lemon juice. Coat the mushroom caps in this mixture and let them marinate overnight in the refrigerator. Add a pinch of salt and pepper onto the mushroom. Place the caps face down on a grill or baking sheet. Grill on medium, bake (350°F (180°C)), or pan sauté on medium heat until cooked, 5 minutes per side (for grill or pan) or 30 minutes in the oven.

2. **To make the garlic mash:** Peel the potatoes and then cut each into 3 or 4 pieces. Boil them until soft, 15 to 20 minutes.

3. Transfer the potato pieces to another pot or just drain them and put them back in the same pot. Add the vegan butter, half-and-half, unsweetened almond milk or soy milk, salt, garlic, and sugar. Smash with a potato smasher, and then whip with an electric mixer until smooth and creamy.

4. Divide the mash between two plates and place the mushroom caps face down on top. Garnish with the sautéed onion and red pepper, micro greens, and Vegan Sweeney Sauce, spooning a generous amount over the mushrooms. Then splatter the sauce around the dish to resemble splattered blood.

Frog's Breath & Nightshade Risotto

PREP TIME: 10 MINUTES | COOK TIME: 30 MINUTES | YIELD: 3–6 SERVINGS

Special thanks to Chef Christoffer Binotto for this wonderfully witchy recipe. Light and springy, this Beetle House Los Angeles original features fresh English peas and a smoked ham hock, along with pea puree and a pea tendril salad in a creamy risotto.

DEADLY INGREDIENTS

PEA PUREE

2 cups (300 g) English peas, blanched

1/4 cup (60 ml) grapeseed/canola oil blend

4 cloves garlic, peeled

Salt, to taste

RISOTTO

1/4 cup (60 ml) grapeseed/canola oil blend

1 1/2 cups (293 g) Arborio rice

1 small shallot, diced

3 cloves garlic, minced

1 cup (235 ml) white wine

3 1/2 cups (820 ml) chicken stock, divided

3 tablespoons salt

1/4 cup (60 ml) (smoked) ham hock, shredded off the bone

2 tablespoons butter

1/4 cup (25 g) grated Parmesan

1/4 cup (38 g) English peas

PEA TENDRIL SALAD

Small bunch pea tendrils

Juice of 1 Meyer lemon

Olive oil, to taste

Salt, to taste

TO MAKE IT

1. **To make the pea puree:** In a blender, add the blanched peas, the oil blend, and peeled garlic cloves. Blend together until smooth, and then add salt to taste.

2. **To make the risotto:** Warm the oil blend in a medium saucepan over medium heat. Add the rice and stir constantly until lightly toasted, about 12 minutes. Add the shallots and garlic to sweat with the rice for about 2 minutes. Deglaze by pouring the white wine into the pan. Once the wine is cooked off, and there is almost no liquid left, then slowly add 3 cups (700 ml) of the chicken stock and stir for about 30 minutes or until the rice is al dente. Remove from saucepan and let cool to room temperature.

3. Heat the cooled risotto with the remaining 1/2 cup (120 ml) chicken stock over medium-low heat for about 1 1/2 minutes. Add the smoked ham hock and fold in the Pea Puree. Continue to stir for a minute or two, then stir in the butter, Parmesan, and English peas.

4. **To make the pea tendril salad:** Mix the pea tendrils with lemon juice, olive oil, and salt to taste.

5. Garnish the risotto with the pea tendril salad. Zest the lemon peel over the dish.

Silence of the Lamb Chops

PREP TIME: 15 MINUTES | COOK TIME: 25 MINUTES | YIELD: 1

This simple, tasty lamb dish was inspired by one of the most iconic horror movies of all time. Make it gory with raspberry glaze splatters and serve with a scalpel instead of a steak knife! Can I interest anyone in some fava beans?

DEADLY INGREDIENTS

MARINADE

¼ cup (60 ml) olive oil

1 clove garlic, crushed

1 sprig rosemary, chopped

½ teaspoon sea salt

¼ cup (60 ml) apple cider

¼ teaspoon black pepper

LAMB

1 bone-in lamb shoulder chop

SAUCE

2 tablespoons butter, salted

½ teaspoon crushed garlic

½ cup (80 g) diced red onion

1 cup (70 g) sliced
   portobello mushrooms

¼ teaspoon chopped rosemary

1 cup (150 g) sliced Granny Smith
   apples (not peeled)

1 cup (235 ml) apple cider, plus
   more as needed (see Tip)

¼ teaspoon sea salt

⅛ teaspoon black pepper

RASPBERRY GLAZE

2 tablespoons seedless
   raspberry preserve

2 tablespoons water

1 tablespoon soy sauce

TO MAKE IT

1. **To make the marinade:** Mix all the marinade ingredients in a bowl. Marinate the lamb chop for 2 to 6 hours before cooking.

2. **To make the lamb:** When ready to cook, remove the lamb chops from the marinade. If using an open-flame grill, place the lamb chop on the grill and cook on medium for 3 to 5 minutes per side. A little char around the edges is preferable. If using a frying pan, place the lamb chop and marinade in the pan, and coat the lamb chop, cooking them on medium heat for 3 to 5 minutes on each side. Remove the lamb chop and set aside.

3. **To make the sauce:** Heat the butter in the frying pan over medium heat until melted. Then add the garlic, onion, mushrooms, rosemary, and apple slices to the pan and sauté for approximately 3 minutes.

4. Add the apple cider, salt, and pepper. Raise the heat to medium-high and cook, stirring often, until the sauce thickens to a syrupy consistency and caramelizes (see Tip).

5. Return the lamb chop to the frying pan and coat with the sauce, turning several times.

6. **To make the raspberry glaze:** Add the ingredients to a small saucepan and heat on medium until the mixture has the consistency of syrup, approximately 5 minutes.

7. To serve, spoon the mushrooms, apples, and onions in the center of the plate. Place the lamb chop on top and drizzle 2 to 3 tablespoons of the sauce over it. Drizzle more glaze around the plate to mimic blood splatters.

TIP Some of the apple cider will cook off in the pan, so if you find it is too thick, add another ¼ cup (60 ml) apple cider to thin it out a bit.

⋅• Big Fish •⋅

PREP TIME: 30 MINUTES | COOK TIME: 30 MINUTES | YIELD: 4 SERVINGS

Masterful Chef Christoffer Binotto created this whimsical gem at our
Beetle House Los Angeles location, and it's like the South meets the
Pacific in a flavor explosion! This pan-seared salmon sits over a colorful
bed of sweet corn succotash, with roasted red bell pepper puree, basil
oil, and micro shiso leaf—a unique Japanese herb that has a similar
flavor profile to herbs like cilantro, basil, and mint.

DEADLY INGREDIENTS

FISH

1 filet of wild salmon
  (6 ounces or 170 g)
1/4 cup (60 ml) grapeseed/
  canola oil blend

SWEET CORN
SUCCOTASH

2 red bell peppers, diced
2 red onions, diced
1/4 cup (60 ml) grapeseed/
  canola oil blend
5 ears yellow corn
1/4 cup (1/2 stick or 55 g)
  of butter, salted
Salt and black pepper,
  to taste

ROASTED RED
PEPPER PUREE

6 red bell peppers
1/2 cup (120 ml) grapeseed/
  canola oil blend
2 tablespoons salt
5 cloves garlic

BASIL OIL

1/2 cup (20 g) basil
1/4 cup (10 g) spinach
2 cups (475 ml) grapeseed/
  canola oil blend

GARNISH

Micro shiso leaf

TO MAKE IT

1. **To make the basil oil:** Drop the basil and spinach in boiling water for 30 seconds. Remove from water and transfer the greens to a bowl of ice water to stop the cooking. Drain and squeeze as much liquid from the greens as possible with your bare hands into the sink. Stir with the oil blend and refrigerate overnight. Then strain through cheesecloth into a plastic container to save for later.

2. **To make the fish:** Preheat the oven to 500°F (260°C). Heat the oil blend in a large, ovenproof pan over medium heat. Add the salmon and sauté until golden brown, about 2 minutes. Flip the salmon and place the pan in the oven for 3 to 5 minutes.

3. **To make the sweet corn succotash:** Sauté the peppers and onions in a pan over medium heat with a small amount of the oil blend for 3 to 4 minutes. Char the corn on the grill, then remove the kernels by slicing down the stalk with your knife. Sauté the corn with the other vegetables for 2 minutes. Stir in the butter, salt, and pepper. Set aside.

4. **To make the roasted red pepper puree:** Lightly coat the peppers in ¼ cup (60 ml) of the oil blend and 1 tablespoon of the salt. Grill each side about 2 minutes, until blackened on both sides. Transfer the peppers to a plastic container, cover with cling wrap, and set aside until they reach room temperature, about 20 minutes. Then gently remove the charred skin with your finger and remove the seeds. Place the peppers in a blender with the remaining ¼ cup (60 ml) oil blend, remaining 1 tablespoon salt, and the garlic, and blend until smooth. Season to taste.

5. Place 3 ounces of succotash in the center of the plate and lay the salmon on top. Drizzle the puree and basil oil over the fish and around the plate. Then garnish with the micro shiso leaf.

꒰ꕤ Love It Pot Pie ꕤ꒱

PREP TIME: 30 MINUTES | COOK TIME: 20 MINUTES | YIELD: 2 SERVINGS

Unlike Mrs. Lovett's suspicious meat pies in *Sweeney Todd,*
our Love It Pot Pie is a sweet and spicy Southern take on that cozy
English classic: chicken pot pie. Still…enjoy with caution.

DEADLY INGREDIENTS

CHICKEN

2 large boneless, skinless chicken breasts

1/4 cup (60 ml) olive oil

1 teaspoon crushed garlic or garlic paste

1/4 cup (60 ml) lemon juice

VEGETABLE SAUCE

2 tablespoons butter, salted

1/2 cup (120 ml) chicken stock

1/2 cup (120 ml) whole milk

1/2 cup (80 g) chopped onion

1/2 cup (65 g) frozen peas

1/2 cup (65 g) chopped carrots

1/2 cup (60 g) chopped red bell peppers

1 cup (235 ml) Love It Sauce (page 16)

1 whole sprig fresh rosemary

1/2 teaspoon finely chopped rosemary

1/2 cup (35 g) chopped cremini mushrooms

HALLOWPEÑO HONEY CHEDDAR CORNBREAD

See page 41, 1 recipe

BEETLE JAM

See page 29, 1/2 teaspoon

TO MAKE IT

1. **To make the chicken:** Marinate the chicken breasts overnight in the olive oil, garlic, and lemon juice. The next day, grill or cook the chicken breast on medium heat in a frying pan or grill until fully cooked, 4 to 6 minutes per side, making sure there is no pink in the meat. Slice or chop the chicken into medium-size chunks or strips.

2. **To make the vegetable sauce:** Add the butter, chicken stock, and milk to a frying pan along with the onion, peas, carrots, and peppers. Stirring frequently, cook on medium heat until the vegetables are fully cooked, 5 to 7 minutes. Add the Love It Sauce and continue stirring until the mixture is smooth and creamy, like an alfredo sauce. (See Tip.) Add the chicken to the sauce. Cook until the sauce is bubbling and thick, another 3 to 5 minutes.

3. Place two pieces of the cornbread at the bottom of each large bowl and top with several spoonfuls of the sauce, until all of the cornbread is covered. Place several pieces of chicken on top of the sauce. Top it all off with the Beetle Jam.

TIP If the sauce is too thick, thin it out with a little milk. If the sauce is too thin, thicken it with a little bit of cornstarch or flour.

Shrimpy Hollow

PREP TIME: 3 HOURS | COOK TIME: 30 MINUTES | YIELD: 2 SERVINGS

Courtesy of Chef Christoffer Binotto, this eclectic dish features sautéed prawns with Hollow Sauce (aka Gochujang Glaze) and a drizzle of chorizo oil on a bed of cheesy corn grits. The scallion oil and micro cilantro add a nice finish, unless you hate cilantro (as you should!) and want to substitute micro basil instead. A fall veggie such as squash or even roasted pumpkin completes the dish!

DEADLY INGREDIENTS

SHRIMP

8 to 10 large prawns (I like U12 prawns), deveined and peeled

2 teaspoons butter, salted

2 teaspoons olive oil

½ teaspoon chopped garlic

Pinch salt

Pinch black pepper

HOLLOW SAUCE

See page 21, to taste

CHEESY CORN GRITS

1 cup (140 g) corn grits

4 cups (950 ml) milk

½ teaspoon salt

¼ cup (½ stick or 55 g) butter, salted

½ cup (40 g) shredded Parmesan cheese

¾ cup (86 g) shredded cheddar cheese

¾ cup (86 g) American cheese

CHORIZO OIL

1½ pounds (680 g) Mexican pork chorizo, fresh, squeezed from casing, and chopped

SCALLION OIL

2 cups (200 g) chopped scallion greens

3 cups (90 g) raw spinach

2 cups (475 ml) grapeseed/canola oil blend

GARNISH

Micro basil (or micro cilantro if you can stomach it).

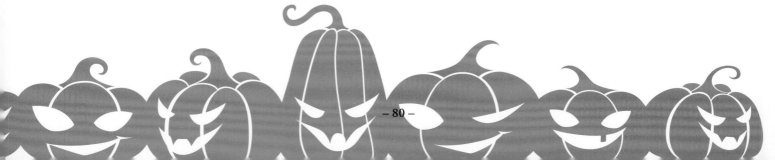

TO MAKE IT

1. **To make the shrimp:** Sauté the shrimp in a pan on medium heat with butter, olive oil, garlic, and a pinch of salt and pepper. Coat with the Hollow Sauce.

2. **To make the cheesy corn grits:** Add the grits, milk, and salt to a pan. While constantly whisking, cook the grits on low to medium heat, until creamy and smooth, 12 to 15 minutes. Mix in the butter and cheeses and stir until melted.

3. **To make the chorizo oil:** Cook the chorizo in a small pot over low heat until fully cooked, 25 to 30 minutes. Strain through a fine-mesh strainer, and then strain again through a cheesecloth, reserving the oil and discarding the meat.

4. **To make the scallion oil:** Drop the scallions and spinach in boiling water for 30 seconds, then remove and transfer to a bowl of ice water to stop the cooking. Drain and squeeze as much liquid as possible from the greens with your hands into the sink. Stir in with the oil blend and, ideally, refrigerate overnight. Then strain through cheesecloth into an airtight plastic container. It will keep in the refrigerator for up to 1 week.

5. Place a hearty amount of the grits in the center of each plate, followed by the shrimp glazed in the Hollow Sauce. Drizzle both oils over the top and garnish with micro basil (or micro cilantro if you don't want me to eat it, see page 35).

Evil Dead Shrimp

PREP TIME: 15 MINUTES | COOK TIME: 10 MINUTES | YIELD: 1 SERVING

Demons and spirits might have been unleashed in the classic cult favorite
The Evil Dead, but in the inspired Beetle House New York, we honor the
movie with a dish that unleashes something else: incredible flavor! Served over
rice and packed with a spicy citrus flavor, come "join us" for a taste.

DEADLY INGREDIENTS

SHRIMP

¼ cup (½ stick or 55 g) butter, salted

1 heaping teaspoon
   crushed garlic or garlic paste

¼ cup (40 g) chopped red onion

¼ cup (33 g) whole-kernel corn

¼ cup (45 g) diced roasted red peppers

½ teaspoon salt

¼ cup (60 ml) lime juice

¼ teaspoon cayenne pepper

¼ cup (60 ml) lobster or chicken stock

1 tablespoon honey

6 to 8 large shrimp or prawns,
   peeled and deveined

RICE

1½ cups (355 ml) water

½ cup (93 g) white rice

1 tablespoon olive oil

1 teaspoon Cajun seasoning

Salt, to taste

GARNISH

Lime slices (or cilantro, but you know how
   I feel about cilantro, see page 35)

TO MAKE IT

1. **To make the shrimp:** In a medium frying pan,
   melt the butter over medium heat. Add the garlic,
   onion, corn, red peppers, and salt and sauté until the
   vegetables are cooked halfway, about 5 to 7 minutes.

2. Add the lime juice, cayenne pepper, stock, honey, and
   shrimp to the pan. Cook on medium-low heat until
   the shrimp are cooked through and the sauce has
   thickened to a medium consistency, about 5 minutes.

3. **To make the rice:** Add the water and rice in a pot
   and cook according to package instructions. Drain
   the rice and transfer it to a large bowl. Stir in the olive
   oil and Cajun seasoning until well combined.

4. Pour the shrimp and sauce mixture over the rice, and
   then toss the ingredients together for about 5 seconds
   Garnish with fresh lime slices. Or cilantro, if you are
   into that shit. Yuck.

Victor Van Pork

PREP TIME: 40 MINUTES | COOK TIME: 6–9 HOURS | YIELD: 8–10 SERVINGS

This is my take on a classic Southern-style pulled pork, jacked up with a bit of heat and some macabre flair. Although this recipe from Beetle House New York City uses two of our signature sauces and the pork requires a lengthy cook time, be reassured that this slow-cooked dish is WORTH IT. Serve this incredible open-faced sandwich with any of your favorite side dishes. We recommend the Garlic Mash (page 66).

DEADLY INGREDIENTS

PORK

2 tablespoons olive oil, divided

1 red onion, finely chopped

3/4 cup (175 ml) water

1 boneless pork shoulder (3 pounds, or 1.4 kg), trimmed of skin and fat

1/2 teaspoon sea salt

1/2 teaspoon black pepper

1 tablespoon chopped garlic

1/2 teaspoon ground cinnamon

1/4 teaspoon chipotle powder

3 tablespoons honey

2 tablespoon soy sauce

1 tablespoon liquid smoke (or other similar smoke flavor)

2 cups (475 ml) Soul Sauce (page 30)

2 tablespoons spicy brown mustard

JALAPEÑO COLESLAW

1 package (14 ounces, or 395 g) coleslaw mix

1 medium jalapeño pepper, seeds removed, finely chopped

1/2 cup (115 g) mayonnaise

2 tablespoons apple cider vinegar

1/4 cup (25 g) sugar

3/4 teaspoon sea salt

1 1/2 tablespoons lemon juice

1/2 teaspoon ground black pepper

1/2 teaspoon smoked paprika

SANDWICH

8 to 10 large kaiser rolls

Veruca Sauce (page 20), to taste

6 red-beet pickled eggs, store-bought

Beetle Jam (page 29)

TO MAKE IT

1. To make the pork: Place 1 tablespoon of the olive oil, the onions, and the water in the bottom of a slow cooker. Rub the remaining 1 tablespoon olive oil all over the pork, along with the salt, pepper, garlic, cinnamon, and chipotle powder. Transfer the pork to the slow cooker and top with the honey, soy sauce, and liquid smoke. Cover and cook on low until very tender, about 8 hours, or on medium for 5 to 6 hours.

2. Remove the meat from the slow cooker. When the meat is cool enough to handle, tear it into thin shreds using two forks, making sure to remove any fat or gristle. Skim any excess fat from the liquid in the slow cooker. Return the pulled pork to the slow cooker and stir in the Soul Sauce and mustard. Cover and cook for another hour on low.

3. To make the jalapeño coleslaw: Place the coleslaw mix and jalapeño in a large bowl. In a small bowl, mix together the remaining ingredients, stirring until fully blended. Pour the dressing over the coleslaw. Mix well and refrigerate until serving.

4. To make the sandwich: Generously brush the insides of the top and bottom of the kaiser rolls with the Veruca Sauce, making sure to cover the insides completely. Then, in a pan or on the grill, toast the rolls (buttered side facing down) until golden brown and slightly crisp, about 2 to 5 minutes.

5. Slice each of the pickled eggs into approximately 5 slices. Place a generous amount of the pulled pork on the bottom buns, followed by the coleslaw and three slices of the pickled egg.

6. On the inside of the top buns, spread a generous amount of the Beetle Jam. Serve the sandwich open-faced, with the top bun face up next to the bottom bun.

Victor Van Mushroom

PREP TIME: 40 MINUTES | COOK TIME: 1½–2 HOURS | YIELD: 8–10 SERVINGS

DEADLY INGREDIENTS

MUSHROOMS

1 pound (454 g) cremini mushrooms

1 pound (454 g) shiitake mushrooms

1 cup (235 ml) Soul Sauce (page 30)

½ cup (120 ml) water

½ onion, chopped

2 tablespoons apple cider vinegar

2 tablespoons brown sugar

3 tablespoons olive oil

JALAPEÑO COLESLAW

1 package (14 ounces, or 395 g)
coleslaw mix

1 medium jalapeño pepper, seeds
removed, finely chopped

½ cup (115 g) vegan mayonnaise

2 tablespoons apple cider vinegar

¼ cup (25 g) sugar

¾ teaspoon sea salt

1½ tablespoons lemon juice

½ teaspoon black pepper

½ teaspoon smoked paprika

VEGAN HONEY BUTTER

¼ cup (60 ml) olive oil

1 teaspoon crushed garlic or garlic paste

1 teaspoon agave nectar

Salt, to taste

SANDWICH

8 to 10 large kaiser rolls

6 pickled red beets

Beetle Jam (page 29)

TO MAKE IT

1. **To make the mushrooms:** Finely slice all mushrooms and add them to a pot with the Soul Sauce, water, onion, vinegar, brown sugar, and olive oil. Mix and cook on medium-low heat, stirring frequently, until the sauce has the consistency of barbecue sauce, 1½ to 2 hours.

   TIP If the sauce is too thick, thin it out with water or more Soul Sauce.

2. **To make the jalapeño coleslaw:** Place the coleslaw mix and jalapeño in a large bowl. In a small bowl, mix together the remaining ingredients, stirring until fully blended. Pour the dressing over the coleslaw. Mix well and refrigerate until serving.

3. **To make the vegan honey butter:** Stir all the ingredients together with a spoon in a small saucepan.

4. **To make the sandwich:** Generously brush the insides of the top and bottom of the kaiser rolls with the Vegan Honey Butter, making sure to cover the insides completely. Then, in a pan or on the grill, toast the rolls (buttered side facing down) until golden brown and slightly crisp, anywhere from 2 to 5 minutes.

5. Slice each of the pickled beets into approximately 5 slices. On the inside of the bottom buns, place a generous amount of the mushroom mixture, followed by the coleslaw and three slices of the pickled beet.

6. On the inside of the top buns, spread a generous amount of the Beetle Jam. Serve the sandwich open-faced, with the top bun face up next to the bottom bun.

CHAPTER

TRICKS & TREATS

DEVILISH DESSERTS

Willy's Mango Panna Cotta

PREP TIME: 30 MINUTES | COOK TIME: 10 MINUTES | YIELD: 4 SERVINGS

A Beetle House Los Angeles original developed by the indominable Chef Christoffer Binotto, this creamy mango panna cotta is topped with passion fruit foam and served with diced kiwi, fresh strawberries, and Cocoa Puffs! Serve in a cool "wonky" goblet, champagne flute, or even a margarita glass. Make a statement with this dessert, just like Willy would have done!

DEADLY INGREDIENTS

PANNA COTTA

2 cups (475 ml) mango juice

1 cup (235 ml) heavy cream

3 tablespoons sugar

1 teaspoon powdered gelatin

PASSION FRUIT FOAM

2 tablespoons soy lecithin (see Tip)

1½ cups (355 ml) passion fruit juice

1 tablespoon heavy cream

1 tablespoon unsalted butter

TOPPING

3 kiwis, diced

6 strawberries, diced

1 cup (27 g) Cocoa Puffs

TO MAKE IT

1. Chill the bowls you will be using to serve the panna cotta in the refrigerator.

2. To make the panna cotta: In a medium saucepan, bring the mango juice to a boil and boil until the juice is reduced by half. Then fold in the cream and bring to a simmer. Simmer for 4 to 5 minutes.

3. Whisk the sugar and gelatin together in a bowl. Then whisk this mixture into the saucepan and let simmer for another 2 minutes. Transfer the liquid from the saucepan into a bowl and whisk every 4 minutes until the mixture cools to room temperature.

4. When the mixture has reached room temperature, pour into your already chilled serving vessels then let them set in the refrigerator for 2 to 3 hours.

5. To make the passion fruit foam: In a bowl, whisk the soy lecithin with just enough water to make it a thick, pasty consistency. In a medium saucepan, bring the passion fruit juice to a boil.

6. Add the cream and butter, and then whisk in the lecithin paste. Let the mixture boil for 1 minute to activate and start forming the foam. Remove from the heat and let cool to room temperature. Finally, transfer the cooled liquid to a blender and blend to emulsify.

7. To make the topping: Top the panna cotta with the diced kiwis and strawberries. Scatter the Cocoa Puffs on top of the panna cotta with the diced fruit, and crown it all off with the passion fruit foam.

TIP Soy lecithin is what helps to create that foam from the passion fruit on top of Willy's Panna Cotta. It's not readily available in all stores, but you can definitely buy it online.

Bloodbath Cobbler

PREP TIME: 30 MINUTES | COOK TIME: 30 MINUTES | YIELD: 8 SERVINGS

My take on a classic cobbler has a bit of a twist. This recipe blends dark cherries and blood oranges to create a bloody, gruesome-looking cobbler, like something you might see served at Mrs. Lovett's shop. Don't let the bloody mess fool you—this cobbler is delicious, especially when served warm with some ice cream! Ready for your close shave? Let's begin.

DEADLY INGREDIENTS

CRUST

1¼ cups (156 g) unbleached all-purpose flour

⅓ cup (67 g) raw sugar

¼ teaspoon sea salt

½ cup (1 stick or 112 g) salted butter, cut into 6 slices

1 egg yolk

2 tablespoons cold water

1 teaspoon vanilla extract

FILLING

12 ounces (340 g) frozen, pitted unsweetened dark cherries

¼ cup (60 ml) agave nectar

1 blood orange, peeled

¼ teaspoon sea salt

2 cups (475 ml) water

½ cup (100 g) raw cane sugar

GO VEGAN! Substitute coconut oil for the butter and a quarter of a mashed banana or a vegan egg substitute for the egg yolk.

TO MAKE IT

1. **To make the crust:** Combine the flour, sugar, and salt in a food processor. Pulse a few times until fully mixed. Add the butter and pulse until the mixture has the texture of a crumb topping; the butter pieces should be larger than small peas.

2. In a mixing bowl, whisk together the egg yolk, cold water, and vanilla. Add the mixture to the food processor and pulse 5 or 6 times until a dough starts to form, being careful not to overmix.

3. Transfer the dough to a sheet of plastic wrap on a flat work surface, such as a countertop or cutting board. Form the dough into a big ball and then smash it down into a disk roughly 8 inches (20 cm) across. Wrap the dough in the plastic and place it in the refrigerator for 25 to 40 minutes.

4. Remove the dough from the refrigerator and roll it out into a flat square about ¼ inch (5 mm) thick. Cut the dough into 3 to 5 strips. Reserve any extra dough crumbles.

5. Preheat the oven to 400°F (200°C).

6. **To make the filling:** Put the cherries and agave nectar into a saucepan and heat on medium-low for 5 minutes. Remove any seeds, if any, from the blood orange. Puree it in a food processor and then add the puree to the cherry mixture.

7. Increase the heat to medium and continue to cook for another 5 to 7 minutes. Then add the water and sugar, continuing to cook for about 15 more minutes, until a medium-thick syrup (the consistency of corn syrup) starts to form. Remove from the heat. (See Tip.)

8. Place two strips of dough and some of the reserved dough crumbles in the bottom of the prepared dish. Pour the berry mix on top. Then take the remaining pieces of dough and cover the top of the berry mix. Bake uncovered for 6 minutes, then reduce the temperature to 350°F (180°C) and cook for another 24 minutes. Remove from the oven and allow to cool for 15 to 20 minutes before serving.

9. Always serve this cobbler warm, ideally on a white plate, and drip a little of the berry syrup around the edges. Garnish the plate with a straight razor (without the blade) and a fake finger or ear, remembering to place it under the cobbler, so it's not seen until your guest starts eating!

TIP If the berry mixture gets too thick, add a little more water. If it is not thick enough after 15 or so minutes, increase the heat slightly and continue to cook a little longer.

 Blood Orange Cheesecake

PREP TIME: 2 HOURS | COOK TIME: 85–95 MINUTES | YIELD: 10-12 SERVINGS

If you've never had a blood orange before, then you're in for a sweet treat. Named for its dark crimson flesh color, this antioxidant-rich fruit lends a bloody, berry tinge to one of Chef Christoffer Binotto's signature desserts. Rich and creamy, this cheesecake is an absolute must for any Halloween-themed bash or just a romantic evening with the vampire in your life.

DEADLY INGREDIENTS

CRUST

2 dozen golden Oreos

4 tablespoons unsalted butter, melted

FILLING

1 cup (200 g) sugar

3 tablespoons cornstarch

3 packages (8 ounces each, or 227 g) cream cheese, softened

5 large eggs

¼ cup (60 g) sour cream

¼ cup (60 ml) heavy cream

Zest and juice of 1 blood orange

GLAZE

3 blood oranges, sliced thinly

½ cup (120 g) water

¾ cup (150 g) sugar

TO MAKE IT

1. Preheat the oven to 400°F (200°C). Grease an 8-inch (20 cm) cheesecake or springform pan with cooking spray. Line the pan with parchment paper and coat it with cooking spray as well.

2. To make the crust: Add the golden Oreos to the food processor and process until all large pieces have been broken up. Transfer the processed Oreos to a bowl and stir in the melted butter. Press the mixture into the bottom of the pan until you form an even layer.

3. To make the filling: In a large mixing bowl, whisk together the sugar and cornstarch. Add the cream cheese, one package at a time, while beating together the ingredients with an electric mixer. Then add the eggs, one at a time, followed by the sour cream, heavy cream, orange zest, and juice. Keep mixing until you have a smooth batter. Transfer the batter to the pan, spreading it on top of the crust.

4. Place the cheesecake pan in a larger pan and fill the larger pan with 1 inch (2.5 cm) of water. This water bath will help prevent the cheesecake from cracking while it bakes.

5. Transfer the pan to the oven and bake the cheesecake for 15 minutes. Then lower the heat to 300°F (150°C) and continue baking for an additional 70 to 80 minutes.

6. Allow the cheesecake to cool down in the oven with the heat off and the door ajar for 1 hour. (Note that the center will still jiggle slightly.) Then place the cheesecake in the refrigerator to chill overnight.

7. To make the glaze: Meanwhile, place the orange slices, water, and sugar in a saucepan and bring the mixture to a simmer. Continue to cook, stirring the mixture occasionally, until the liquid is thick and syrupy, about 20 minutes. Pour the glaze into a plastic container and refrigerate. Take out orange slices and dip them into a sugar, then put them into a plastic container and store until cheesecake is done.

8. In the morning, transfer the cheesecake to a serving platter and top with the glaze.

Beetle Pie

The colors and textures of this pie are inspired by one of my all-time favorite films, *Beetlejuice*. I wanted the look of it alone to somehow remind you of Tim Burton and his marvelous, memorable goth-com. The brilliant green color of the homemade pistachio pudding and the crunchy chocolate crust evoke the corpse-fed grass and rich soil of a graveyard, while the seedy and sweet blackberry jam mimics the texture of blood and bugs. You can store the pie, covered, in the refrigerator for up to a week, but it is best served within 12 to 24 hours. Rich, thick, and creepily delicious, Beetle Pie is a perfect dessert for any occasion for pistachio lovers—but we of course recommend it for Halloween.

DEADLY INGREDIENTS

CRUST

35 chocolate cookie wafers

¼ cup (½ stick or 55 g) salted butter, melted and cooled to room temperature

FILLING

¼ cup (92 g) roasted salted shelled pistachios

⅔ cup (133 g) raw sugar, divided

2 tablespoons water

½ teaspoon vanilla extract

2 cups (475 ml) whole milk

2 large egg yolks

2 tablespoons cornstarch

pinch of salt

2 tablespoons unsalted butter

Green food coloring or food dye

BLACKBERRY JAM

1 cup (145 g) fresh blackberries

2 cups (475 ml) water

1 cup (200 g) raw cane sugar

TOPPING

1 cup (40 g) whipped topping, preferably Cool Whip

6 to 8 whole fresh blackberries

TO MAKE IT

1. To make the crust: Preheat the oven to 350°F (180°C).

2. Place the cookie wafers into a food processor and pulse until the crumbs are about the size of peas. Add the melted butter and continue to process until the consistency is like coffee grounds.

3. Transfer the crumbs to a 9-inch (23 cm) pie plate. Use a cup or your hands to firmly press the crumbs evenly into the bottom and sides of the pan. Bake until fragrant, 10 to 15 minutes. Remove and cool completely before filling.

4. To make the filling: Place the pistachios into the food processor. Add ⅓ cup (67 g) of the sugar. Pulse until the nuts and sugar are as close to the consistency of powder as you can get. Add the water and pulse until the mixture becomes a paste.

5. In a medium saucepan, whisk together the pistachio paste, vanilla extract, and milk over medium heat until the mixture just starts to boil slightly. Then remove it from the heat.

6. In a separate mixing bowl, whisk together the remaining ⅓ cup (66 g) sugar, the egg yolks, cornstarch, and salt. Continue whisking until you have a smooth yellow paste. Add the egg mixture to the milk mixture and return to medium heat, whisking frequently until the pudding starts to boil. Whisk for another 30 to 60 seconds, until the pudding thickens fully, then remove from the heat.

7. Stir in the butter until it is melted and blended with the pudding. Add 2 to 3 drops of green food coloring or green food dye to get a brilliant green color. Transfer the pudding to a container with a lid and place in the refrigerator for 2 to 3 hours, or until cold.

8. To make the blackberry jam: Place the fresh blackberries, water, and sugar into a medium saucepan. Heat on medium for approximately 20 minutes, stirring frequently and using a whisk to break up the berries. Continue to heat and stir until a medium-thick syrup has formed. Remove from the heat.

9. Using a spatula, pour the cold pudding into the pie crust. Fill the crust to about 2 inches (5 cm) below the top of the crust edge. Use the spatula to make sure the mixture is spread evenly.

10. Using another spatula, dab a large helping of jam (about the diameter of a DVD and ¼ inch or 5 mm thick) into the center of the pie. Using the same spatula, drip more jam in random places around the edges and other areas of the pie (think blood spatter).

11. Place the whipped topping directly in the center of the pie. Use a spatula to create peaks and valleys in the whipped topping so that it resembles a cloud. Finish the dessert by sticking the whole blackberries in the whipped topping in random places to resemble bugs.

12. Serve the pie on a white plate and garnish with small plastic beetles and/or spiders dipped in the blackberry jam. Refrigerate the plates with the bugs and pie on them for an hour before serving.

GO VEGAN! Substitute vegan chocolate cookies, plain or vanilla almond milk, and vegan whipped cream (such as So Delicious CocoWhip). Use coconut oil in place of the butter and half a banana or a vegan egg substitute in place of the egg yolks.

Red Velvet Midnight Espresso Cake with Stained-Glass Candy Shards

PREP TIME: 2 HOURS | COOK TIME: 33–38 MINUTES | YIELD: 10–12 SERVINGS

Don't let the red velvet fool you…this rich, decadent cake is a must for chocolate and candy lovers. Topped with candy shards and a sweet raspberry sauce, you'll punch through a stained-glass window to have this cake.

DEADLY INGREDIENTS

CAKE

4 ounces (115 g) semisweet chocolate, chopped

2 cups (240 g) sifted cake flour

1/2 cup (42 g) unsweetened cocoa powder

1 teaspoon baking powder

1/2 teaspoon salt

1 1/2 cups (340 g) packed light brown sugar

1 cup (2 sticks or 225 g) unsalted butter, softened

4 large eggs

1 teaspoon vanilla extract

1 cup (235 ml) brewed espresso

10 drops red food coloring

3/4 cup (175 ml) buttermilk

1 cup (320 g) apricot or seedless raspberry jam

Whipped cream, for serving

RASPBERRY SAUCE

3/4 cup (150 g) granulated sugar

3/4 cup (175 ml) water

4 tablespoons cornstarch

4 cups fresh or frozen raspberries

GANACHE

10 ounces (285 ml) semisweet chocolate, chopped

1 cup (235 ml) heavy cream

STAINED-GLASS CANDY SHARDS

1 cup (100 g) confectioner's sugar

1 cup (235 ml) water

3 1/2 cups (700 g) granulated sugar

1 cup (235 ml) light corn syrup

1 tablespoon red food coloring

2 teaspoons raspberry- or cinnamon-flavored extract

TO MAKE IT

1. To make the cake: Preheat the oven to 350°F (180°C). Grease the bottoms of two 8-inch (20 cm) round cake pans with cooking spray and line the bottoms with parchment paper.

2. In a saucepan, melt the semisweet chocolate in a double boiler over low heat and then let it cool to room temperature. Meanwhile, sift the flour, cocoa, baking powder, and salt into a small bowl.

3. Using a stand mixer or a hand mixer, blend the brown sugar, butter, eggs, vanilla, and espresso in a large bowl for 3 minutes. Gradually add in the melted chocolate and food coloring as you mix. Then add in the flour mixture and buttermilk, mixing on a low setting until smooth.

4. Pour the mixture into the prepared pans, transfer to the oven, and bake until the cake springs back when touched, 33 to 38 minutes. Allow the cakes to cool in the pan for 10 minutes, and then invert the cakes onto a cooling rack to cool completely.

5. To make the sauce: Combine the sugar, water, and cornstarch in a small saucepan. Cook on medium heat until it simmers, and then add the raspberries. Cook until the raspberries break down, about 4 minutes. Once the mixture has a syrupy texture, strain it through a fine-mesh strainer to remove the pulp and seeds.

6. To make the ganache: Place the chopped chocolate in a medium bowl. Pour the heavy cream into a saucepan and heat until it simmers. Then pour the heated cream over the chocolate in the bowl and let sit for a few minutes. Finally, whisk the cream and chocolate together until the chocolate melts and the mixture is smooth.

7. To make the stained-glass candy shards: Line a baking sheet or baking pan with foil and sift the confectioner's sugar over the entire pan. In a heavy-bottomed pot, add the water, granulated sugar, and corn syrup. Stir to start dissolving sugar and then turn heat up to medium and let the sugar dissolve on its own. Wet a pastry brush and brush down the crystals that form on the side of the pot or else the sauce will turn gritty. Once the sugar dissolves, insert a candy thermometer and bring the mixture to a boil. Don't stir the mixture while boiling.

8. When the temperature reaches 300°F (150°C), remove the pot from the heat and add the food coloring and extract, stirring to combine. Pour the candy mixture onto the foil-lined pan, tilting it to spread out the mixture. Cool for at least 1 hour.

9. Once the mixture has cooled, take a mallet and crack the mixture into pieces (they can be randomly sized). Then shake off the excess confectioner's sugar and store the shards in plastic containers.

10. Once the cakes have cooled, spread some of the raspberry sauce over the bottom layer and then top with the second layer. Starting in the center, pour the cooled ganache over the cake, and use a spatula to smooth the chocolate all over the outside of it.

11. To decorate, stick the stained glass candy shards into the top of the cake. Serve with whipped cream and the remaining raspberry sauce.

TIP While the candy is cooling, place it on a trivet. The bottom of the pan gets really hot and may burn the counter.

Boozy Mango Sorbet with Pop Rocks

PREP TIME: 40 MINUTES | YIELD: 6 CUPS

This candy-covered frozen treat is an explosion of sweetness—literally. The alcohol content adds another layer of fun, so, in true Halloween fashion, get ready to chill, thrill, and startle your party guests with this creamy concoction.

DEADLY INGREDIENTS

4 ripe mangoes
1 cup (235 ml) simple syrup (See page 106)
3 tablespoons fresh lime juice, or to taste
4 fl oz (120 ml) peach-flavored vodka
Pop Rocks (for serving)

TO MAKE IT

1. Wash and dry the mangoes. Then, using a sharp knife, remove their skins. Cut away the flesh lengthwise, as close to the pit as possible.

2. Place the mango slices into a blender, along with the simple syrup, lime juice, and vodka. Puree the ingredients.

3. Transfer the mixture into an ice cream or sorbet machine. Every machine is different, so the time may vary, but the sorbet is usually set up in 20 to 30 minutes.

4. Place the sorbet in a container and let freeze overnight.

5. When ready to serve, scoop the sorbet into a bowl and sprinkle with Pop Rocks.

TIP For a smooth, chunk-free sorbet, pass the mango puree through a strainer before placing it in your sorbet or ice cream maker.

CHAPTER 6

POISONS, POTIONS & ELIXIRS

DEADLY DRINKS, CREEPY COCKTAILS

The Beetle's Juice

YIELD: 1 SERVING

You're in for a treat with this creepy concoction of sour cranberry juice and sweet blackberry schnapps created by Beetle House mixologist Gia Farrell.

DEADLY INGREDIENTS

2 blackberries
1 slice lime
½ ounce (15 ml) simple syrup (see Tip)
1½ ounces (45 ml) silver tequila
1 dash angostura bitters
½ ounce (15 ml) lime juice
½ ounce (15 ml) blackberry schnapps
2 ounces (60 ml) cranberry juice

SERVING VESSEL

Highball glass

GARNISH

1 lime wheel
1 blackberry

TO MAKE IT

1. In a pint glass, muddle the blackberries, lime slice, and simple syrup.

2. Fill a cocktail shaker halfway with ice. Then add the tequila, angostura bitters, lime juice, blackberry schnapps, cranberry juice, and the muddled ingredients.

3. Shake the ingredients for about 5 seconds.

4. Dump the drink straight into the highball glass and garnish with the lime wheel and blackberry.

GO VIRGIN! This drink can be made non-alcoholic by substituting cranberry juice for the silver tequila and schnapps.

TIP You can make your own simple syrup by combining 1½ cups of water with 1 cup of sugar and bringing them to a boil or until they form a syrupy consistency.

The Golden Ticket

YIELD: 1 SERVING

You've finally found your Golden Ticket! This pretty cocktail is cause for celebration indeed. Whipped vodka, tequila rose, and almond milk are just a few of the lip-smacking ingredients in this gorgeous drink. It's the perfect complement to an outrageous birthday dinner or a super sweet treat after a bad day. Now back to working on the recipe for those fizzy-lifting drinks...

DEADLY INGREDIENTS

1½ ounces (45 ml) whipped vodka
1 ounce (30 ml) tequila rose
1 ounce (30 ml) almond milk
½ ounce (15 ml) simple syrup (see page 106)
½ ounce (15 ml) lime juice
¼ ounce (7.5 ml) curaçao
Whipped cream, nondairy whipped cream

SERVING VESSEL

Collins glass

GARNISH

Cotton candy
Nerds candy
Candy of your choice

TO MAKE IT

1. Fill a Collins glass with ice.

2. Add ice to a cocktail shaker. Then add whipped vodka, tequila rose, almond milk, simple syrup, and lime juice. Shake for about 5 seconds.

3. Pour into Collins glass. Top with the curaçao.

4. Top with nondairy whipped cream, cotton candy, and Nerds.

5. Garnish with a side of candy of your choosing.

Edward's Lemonade

YIELD: 1 SERVING

During *Edward Scissorhands*, Edward gets a dose of Bill's favorite drink, which he not-so-innocently calls "lemonade." Here is mixologist Gia Farrell's interpretation of Bill's concoction: an old-fashioned with a fruity twist! Sip it through a straw just like Edward and your eyes will water too.

DEADLY INGREDIENTS

2 maraschino cherries
1 orange slice
½ ounce (15 ml) simple syrup (see page 106)
3 ounces (90 ml) bourbon
1 dash orange bitters

SERVING VESSEL

Rocks glass

GARNISH

1 slice orange
1 maraschino cherry

TO MAKE IT

1. In a pint glass, muddle the cherries, orange slice, and simple syrup.

2. Fill a cocktail shaker halfway with ice. Then add the bourbon, orange bitters, and the muddled ingredients.

3. With a spoon, stir all the ingredients in the shaker for about 5 seconds.

4. Add one large square ice cube to a rocks glass and strain the drink into it. Garnish with the orange slice and cherry.

❧ The Fleet Street Martini ❧

YIELD: 1 SERVING

If you're normally sweet but feeling a little spicy tonight, you're going to love this bright-red martini featuring Fireball Cinnamon Whiskey! Pair with the equally gory Love It Pot Pie (page 78) of course! Everyone's favorite demon barber would approve.

DEADLY INGREDIENTS

1½ ounces (45 ml) Fireball Cinnamon Whiskey
1 ounce (30 ml) DeKuyper Sour Apple Pucker
1½ ounces (45 ml) cranberry juice

SERVING VESSEL

Martini glass

SUGAR RIM AND GARNISH

Cranberry infused sugar (see Tip)
Lime juice
1 maraschino cherry

TO MAKE IT

1. **To make the sugar rim:** Pour the cranberry red sugar onto a small plate. Fill another small plate with the lime juice. Dip the rim of the martini glass into the lime juice and then into the sugar.

2. Fill a cocktail shaker halfway with ice. Add the whiskey, Sour Apple Pucker, and cranberry juice.

3. Shake the ingredients for about 5 seconds.

4. Strain into the rimmed martini glass and place a skewered cherry across the top.

TIP If cranberry-infused rimming sugar isn't available at your grocery or liquor store, you can buy it online.

Big Fish Bowl

YIELD: 1 SERVING

Inspired by Burton's whimsical *Big Fish*, this show-stopper drink is a must-have for parties. Create the look of an actual mini fish tank with your favorite candies like Nerds and Swedish Fish, and fill your tank with everything your sugary friends need to survive, like tequila, vodka, gin, and Curaçao. Need we say more?

DEADLY INGREDIENTS

1 1.65 ounce box of Nerds candy
1 ounce (30 ml) coconut rum
1 ounce (30 ml) vodka
1 ounce (30 ml) tequila
1 ounce (30 ml) gin
1 ounce (30 ml) Curaçao
1 ounce (30 ml) triple sec
2 ounces (60 ml) pineapple juice
1 ounce (30 ml) sour mix
1 can (12 ounces, or 350 ml)
  Sprite, as needed
5 pieces of Swedish Fish

SERVING VESSEL

1 fishbowl (6 inches, or 15 cm)

GARNISH

1 lemon wheel
1 lime wheel

TO MAKE IT

1. Add the Nerds to the fishbowl, then fill it to the top with ice.

2. Fill a cocktail shaker halfway with ice. Then add the coconut rum, vodka, tequila, gin, Curaçao, triple sec, pineapple juice, and sour mix.

3. Shake the ingredients for about 5 seconds and strain into the fishbowl.

4. Add Sprite to the fishbowl until it is nearly full. Then add a few Swedish Fish.

5. Garnish with the lemon and lime wheels. Serve with a straw!

This Is Halloween

YIELD: 1 SERVING

With autumnal flavors like cinnamon, apple, pumpkin, and ginger, this drink is like fall in your mouth! A terrific cocktail for Halloween parties, Thanksgiving celebrations, or a Friday night treat for all of your pumpkin-obsessed friends who eagerly devour pumpkin spice everything!

DEADLY INGREDIENTS

1½ ounces (45 ml) Fireball
  Cinnamon Whiskey
½ ounce (15 ml) DeKuyper Sour Apple Pucker
½ ounce (15 ml) pumpkin liqueur
1 ounce (30 ml) apple cider
Ginger beer

SERVING VESSEL

Rocks glass

GARNISH

1 lime wheel

TO MAKE IT

1. Fill a cocktail shaker halfway with ice. Then add the whiskey, Sour Apple Pucker, pumpkin liqueur, and apple cider.

2. Shake the ingredients for about 5 seconds.

3. Dump the drink into a rocks glass and top with ginger beer.

4. Garnish with the lime wheel.

•.. Alice's Cup of Tea ..•

YIELD: 1 SERVING

Mixologist Gia Farrell created this fun, peachy concoction for our popular cocktail menu at the Beetle House. Inspired by Lewis Carroll's intrepid Alice, it's what a Long Island Iced Tea would taste like in Wonderland. Drink me, indeed!

DEADLY INGREDIENTS

½ ounce (15 ml) peach vodka

½ ounce (15 ml) gin

½ ounce (15 ml) silver rum

½ ounce (15 ml) silver tequila

½ ounce (15 ml) peach schnapps

1 ounce (30 ml) sour mix

Splash cola

SERVING VESSEL

Highball glass

GARNISH

1 lemon wheel

TO MAKE IT

1. Fill a cocktail shaker halfway with ice and add the peach vodka, gin, rum, tequila, peach schnapps, and sour mix.

2. Shake the ingredients for about 5 seconds.

3. Dump the drink into a highball glass and top with a splash of cola.

4. Garnish with the lemon wheel.

The Franken-Martini

YIELD: 1 SERVING

Inspired by Tim Burton's *Frankenweenie*, which was shot entirely in black and white, this decadent martini combines vanilla vodka with a double chocolate liqueur for a boozy milkshake taste! Developed by Beetle House mixologist Gia Farrell, this indulgent drink is a date favorite!

DEADLY INGREDIENTS

2 ounces (60 ml) vanilla vodka

1 ounce (30 ml) Dorda Double
  Chocolate Liqueur

½ ounce (15 ml) whole milk

½ ounce (15 ml) crème de coco

SERVING VESSEL

Martini glass

GARNISH

Whipped cream

Chocolate syrup

Chocolate bar

TO MAKE IT

1. Fill a cocktail shaker halfway with ice. Add the vodka, chocolate liqueur, milk, and crème de coco.

2. Shake the ingredients for about 5 seconds.

3. Strain into a martini glass. Garnish with the whipped cream, chocolate syrup, and a chocolate bar.

The Nine

A neon-green appletini on steroids.
If you like your 'tini extra sweet, add a sugared rim!

DEADLY INGREDIENTS

1 ounce (30 ml) citrus vodka
1 ounce (30 ml) DeKuyper
  Sour Apple Pucker
½ ounce (15 ml) Midori
½ ounce (15 ml) triple sec

SERVING VESSEL

Martini glass

SUGAR RIM AND GARNISH

Sour apple sugar (see Tip)
Lime juice
1 maraschino cherry

TO MAKE IT

1. **To make the sugar rim:** Pour the green sugar onto a small plate. Fill another small plate with the lime juice. Dip the rim of the martini glass into the lime juice and then into the green sugar.

2. Fill a cocktail shaker halfway with ice. Add the vodka, Sour Apple Pucker, Midori, and triple sec.

3. Shake the ingredients for about 5 seconds.

4. Strain into the rimmed martini glass and garnish with the cherry.

TIP If sour apple sugar for your cocktail rim isn't available at your grocery or liquor store, you can buy it online.

We Come in Peace

Just like those pesky aliens in *Mars Attacks*, this creamy drink is tough to figure out—a perfect blend of sweet and salty, it's the kind of irresistibly dangerous drink that you'll consistently underestimate…until it's too late.

DEADLY INGREDIENTS

1½ ounces (45 ml) Stoli
  Salted Karamel vodka
1½ ounces (45 ml) RumChata
Whole milk
Caramel syrup

SERVING VESSEL

Martini glass

SALTED RIM AND GARNISH

Salt
Whipped cream
Caramel syrup

TO MAKE IT

1. **To make the salted rim:** Pour salt onto a small plate and fill another plate with water. First dip the rim of the martini glass into the water and then into the salt.

2. Fill a cocktail shaker halfway with ice. Add the vodka, RumChata, a splash of milk, and a drizzle of caramel syrup.

3. Shake the ingredients for about 5 seconds.

4. Strain into the rimmed martini glass and garnish with whipped cream and a drizzle of caramel syrup.

Sparky's Minty Margarita

YIELD: 1 SERVING

You like margaritas? You like mojitos?
In this drink you get the best of both worlds!
Let this drink spark up your evening.

DEADLY INGREDIENTS

1 lime slice
3 mint leaves
½ ounce (15 ml) simple syrup (see page 106)
1½ ounces (45 ml) silver tequila
½ ounce (15 ml) Grand Marnier
½ ounce (15 ml) sour mix
Club soda

SERVING VESSEL

Highball glass

GARNISH

1 lime wheel
1 mint leaf

TO MAKE IT

1. In a pint glass, muddle the lime, mint leaves, and simple syrup.

2. Fill a cocktail shaker halfway with ice. Then add the tequila, Grand Marnier, sour mix, and muddled ingredients.

3. Shake the ingredients for about 5 seconds.

4. Dump the drink into a highball glass and top with a splash of club soda.

5. Garnish with the lime wheel and mint leaf.

Bio-Exorcism

YIELD: 1 SERVING

If all that human contact and adulting has gotten you down, then you need a bio-exorcism! Created by Beetle House mixologist Gia Farrell, this drink is designed to clear even the most unsavory personalities from your memory (at least temporarily). And who wouldn't feel refreshed with a drink that combines the cool flavors of cucumber and lime with club soda and gin?

DEADLY INGREDIENTS

2 thin slices cucumber
1 slice lime
Lime juice
1 1/2 ounces (45 ml)
  Hendrick's gin
Club soda

SERVING VESSEL

Rocks glass

GARNISH

1 slice cucumber
1 lime wheel

TO MAKE IT

1. In a pint glass, muddle the cucumbers, lime, and a splash of lime juice.

2. Fill a cocktail shaker halfway with ice. Add the gin and muddled ingredients.

3. Shake the ingredients for about 5 seconds.

4. Dump the drink into a rocks glass and top with club soda.

5. Garnish with the cucumber slice and lime wheel.

☩ The Coco Skellington ☩

YIELD: 1 SERVING

Who cares if your skin is whiter than a ghost's and your favorite color, mood, and general temperament is black? It doesn't mean you don't occasionally want to feel like you're on a beach somewhere away from it all. So if your favorite gothic beach is closed (or nonexistent), then Gia Farrell's Coco Skellington is like sitting on your very own gothic beach. And just like Jack, you'll be king!

DEADLY INGREDIENTS

1 ounce (30 ml) silver rum
1 ounce (30 ml) gin
1 ounce (30 ml) crème de coconut
½ ounce (15 ml) lime juice
Small dash of orange bitters
Zest of 1 orange

TO MAKE IT

1. Fill a cocktail shaker halfway with ice. Add the rum, gin, crème de coconut, lime juice, and orange bitters.

2. Shake the ingredients for about 5 seconds.

3. Pour the drink into a highball glass

4. Put extra ice in a separate cup and crush it with a muddler. Then put the crushed ice on top of the drink.

5. Garnish with the orange zest.

CHAPTER 7

PUT THE FUN BACK IN FUNERAL

THEMED PARTIES

Willy's Candy Bar

This technicolor sugar party is all kinds of strange and wonderful. Throw it in the spring or summer, placing different types of candy in jars of all shapes and sizes. Make it a more formal affair with candelabras, fancy napkins, and a few Victorian-style accessories, or nix the place settings and invite the whole neighborhood to celebrate a birthday or other milestone in the sweetest way possible.

MENU

APPETIZER
Charlie Corn Bucket
Giant Peach Salad

MAIN COURSE
The Willy Burger

DESSERT
Willy's Mango Panna Cotta

COCKTAIL SPECIAL
The Golden Ticket

SUGGESTED PROPS & ACCESSORIES

THESE PRODUCTS ARE PERFECT FOR A
WILLY-THEMED CANDY BAR!

Whimsical candy jars

Purple vases

Purple tablecloth

White flatware

Gray and white napkins

Antique utensils

Black top hat with a purple ribbon

Beetle Halloween Party

I have thrown this awesome party several times in my own home, and it is so much fun! Of course, you should cook one of your favorite dishes from this book, have the Beetle's Juice cocktail on hand, and absolutely finish off the night with the Beetle Pie.

MENU

APPETIZER

The Deetz Shrimp Cocktail
Beetle Bacon Bread

MAIN COURSE

Silence of the Lamb Chops
Graveyard Noodles

DESSERT

Beetle Pie

COCKTAIL SPECIAL

The Beetle's Juice

SUGGESTED PROPS & ACCESSORIES

My team and I assembled this list of products to transform your dining room into the ultimate *Beetle*-themed Halloween party.

Black and white striped tablecloth

Black bowls

Black goblet glassware

Red votive candles

Purple napkins

Purple Calla lilies centerpiece

Edward's Formal Dinner Party

I love this party! Think about the pastel colors and the over-the-top 1980s hairstyles from the original movie. This party works anytime in the year, but it is especially fun to throw during the spring, summer, and fall months. You definitely have to serve Edward Burger Hands and Edward's Lemonade for this one!

MENU

APPETIZER

Diablo's Arenas Crostini
Barbarous BBQ Beef Ramen

MAIN COURSE

Edward Burger Hands
French Fries with Edward Sauce

DESSERT

Boozy Mango Sorbet with Pop Rocks

COCKTAIL SPECIAL

Edward's Lemonade

SUGGESTED PROPS & ACCESSORIES

HERE ARE SOME EXCELLENT
'80S-INSPIRED TABLE ACCESSORIES
THAT WILL HELP GET YOU OUTFITTED
FOR YOUR PARTY. DON'T FORGET THE
TOPIARY AND SCISSORS!

Black leather tablecloth

Silver confetti

Pastel blue and pink napkins

Knives: scissor blades

White plates

Whiskey glasses

Green topiary centerpiece with
scissors sticking out

Paper cutouts as table decorations

Nightmare Christmas Party

If it were up to me, I would have this party at my house every Saturday starting from Thanksgiving weekend until New Year's Day! Serve This is Halloween cocktails because it just makes sense. Viva la Halloween!

APPETIZER

Hallowpeño Honey Cheddar Cornbread
Sriracha-Roasted Butternut Squash Death Soup

MAIN COURSE

Frog's Breath & Nightshade Risotto
Shrimpy Hollow

DESSERT

Red Velvet Midnight Espresso Cake with
Stained-Glass Candy Shards

COCKTAIL SPECIAL

This Is Halloween
The Coco Skellington

SUGGESTED PROPS & ACCESSORIES

Use these products to set the scene for the ultimate Nightmare Christmas Party at home. I also recommend loading up your house and Christmas tree with as much Jack paraphernalia as possible!

Light gray ceramic plates with
thin black line patterns and circles

Bright yellow napkins

Light gray ceramic cups with
thin black line patterns and circles

Flatware with black curly stems

Black spiderweb tablecloth

Pumpkin decor

About Beetle House

Beetle House is the year-round celebration of Halloween embodied into a restaurant and bar. The atmosphere and style pay tribute to its many inspirations from the works of Tim Burton, horror culture, and all things dark and lovely. Guests of Beetle House enjoy an eclectic menu of themed food and drinks while being entertained by a cast of characters and performers. Beetle House provides a fun and safe environment where everyone is welcome to come and be their true selves. Beetle house is the place where you can express yourself, dress up, become a character, release your inhibitions, and let your freak flag fly high and proud. Come as you are, come as you want to be, take a taste of the dark side, because at Beetle House, every day is Halloween.

Beetle House NYC
308 E. 6th Street
New York, NY 10003

Beetle House LA
6536 Hollywood Blvd
Los Angeles, CA 90028

MORE LOCATIONS COMING SOON!

ACKNOWLEDGMENTS

I'd like to express my sincere gratitude to the following people:

To my mother, my all-time favorite cook, and the person who could always make something from nothing. Thanks for many years of tasty meals which inspired me to cook myself, and some of the dishes in this book were heavily influenced by your classic recipes.

Chef Christopher Binotto, for Beetle House Los Angeles additional kitchen ops, plating, recipes, and support. Chris, you are my rockstar, thank you.

Gia Farrell for cocktail recipes, set design, and creative direction. We couldn't have done it without you. Thanks for all your help.

Jessica Liu, admin director, and for all your help with editing and shopping. Thank you Jess.

Jeanne Bocchicchio for the additional dessert recipes and support. Thank you.

Richard Lillard for additional set design. Thank you.

As it goes with everything, a person can only be as good as their team and the company they keep. I am very lucky to have been surrounded by some of the absolute best people whom have helped me greatly. In no particular order...

Tim, Freddy, Spencer, Gabriel, Daniela, Violet, Victoria, Lucy, Jessica, the Freak Show Deluxe, Chef Dylan, Dan, Alan, Dakota, Crystal, Walter, Kate, Fatima, unique, Brian, Erika, all my supportive and amazing customers and friends in NYC and LA thank you for being part of my dream.

And finally, a special thank you to the following companies:

New Gold Empire (home to my team)

The Bearded Lady Vintage and Oddities in Burbank, California

Halloween Town in Burbank, California

Boulevard Nightlife Group

TCL Chinese Theater

The Sweet Shop in Hollywood

Southern Wine and Spirits

Beetle House Recipe Credits

Special thanks to **Chef Christoffer Binotto** for his work concocting the following recipes:

Hollow Sauce (page 21)
Giant Peach Salad (page 53)
Frog's Breath & Nightshade Risotto (page 70)
Big Fish (page 75)
Willy's Mango Panna Cotta (page 91)

I'd also like to thank the Beetle House mixologist **Gia Farrell** for her perfect potions including:

The Beetle's Juice (page 106)
The Golden Ticket (page 108)
Edward's Lemonade (page 110)
Big Fish Bowl (page 112)
Alice's Cup of Tea (page 117)
The Franken-Martini (page 118)
The Nine (page 121)
We Come In Peace (page 122)
Sparky's Minty Margarita (page 124)
The Bio-Exorcism (page 125)
The Coco Skellington (page 127)

And finally, thank you to **Jeannie Bocchicchio** for crafting these sweet treats:

Red Velvet Midnight Espresso Cake with Stained Glass Candy Shards (page 99)
Blood Orange Cheesecake (page 94)

About the Author

ZACH NEIL is an American entrepreneur, artist, and chef. He has been featured multiple times on the *Food Network* and has gained additional notoriety through his popular chains of themed restaurants which have been featured on *Watch What Happens Live with Andy Cohen*, *Good Day New York*, *MSNBC*, and *ABC World News Tonight*, among others. Zach combined his artistic pursuits with his culinary skills to create the eclectic, Halloween-themed Beetle House restaurants which have broken media records in the restaurant space. The celebrated menu caught the attention of the Quarto Publishing Group, who collaborated with Neil on his first cookbook, *The Nightmare Before Dinner: Recipes to Die For,* which features all of the Beetle House recipes plus a selection of brand new, never-before-seen dishes with seasonally-inspired flavors and a dash of Gothic insanity. In addition to his restaurant franchises, Neil is considered an authority on pop-up bars and restaurants, with his own television programming and lifestyle brands in the works. You can find Zach on Instagram @therealzachneil and don't forget to check out beetlehouseny.com or beetlehousela.com to find out more about a Beetle House location near you.

Index